WJEC Level 1/2 Vocational Award

Hospitality & Catering

If you want to ace the WJEC Vocational Award in Hospitality and Catering, you need to know your onions (literally and figuratively). And this CGP book is here to help!

It guides you through all the different question types you could face in the Unit 1 exam, and has lots of realistic practice questions to help you prepare.

We've also included fully worked answers to check how you've done and see how to improve — perfect for making sure you're ready for the real thing. Easy as pie!

Unlock your Online Edition

Just scan the QR code below or go to **cgpbooks.co.uk/extras** and enter this code!

3735 0063 9393 4559

By the way, this code only works for one person. If somebody else has used this book before you, they might have already claimed the code.

Exam Practice Workbook

Contents

Exam Skills 1

Section 1 — Topic-based Questions

1.1 — Hospitality and Catering Provision

1.2 — How Providers Operate

1.3 — Health & Safety

1.4 — Food Safety

Exam Skills 2

Section 2 — Mixed Questions

Published by CGP

Editors: Fi Cooley, Liam Dyer, Sharon Keeley-Holden, Christopher Lindle

Contributor: Sarah Mann
Reviewers: Jennifer Bruce, Joanna Phillips

With thanks to Sharon Keeley-Holden and Camilla Sheridan for the proofreading.
With thanks to Jade Sim for the copyright research.

ISBN: 978 1 83774 1458
Printed by Elanders Ltd, Newcastle upon Tyne.
Graphics from Getty PA

Text, design, layout and original illustrations © Coordination Group Publications Ltd. (CGP) 2024
All rights reserved.

Based on the classic CGP style created by Richard Parsons.

Photocopying this book is not permitted, even if you have a CLA licence.
Extra copies are available from CGP with next day delivery. • 0800 1712 712 • www.cgpbooks.co.uk

Short-Answer Questions

You'll sit a **1 hour 20 minute** written exam that's worth **80 marks**. It counts for **40%** of your total grade.

The exam will start off with some **short-answer questions**. They're usually worth up to 4 marks and often begin with one of these **command words**:

- Identify / Place
- Give / Name / List
- Outline
- State
- Describe
- Explain

You'll see these types of questions in both Section 1 and Section 2 of the book.

'Identify...' or 'Place...' questions are usually multiple-choice

For '**Identify**' or '**Place**' questions, you just need to **pick out** or **sort** the **correct information**.

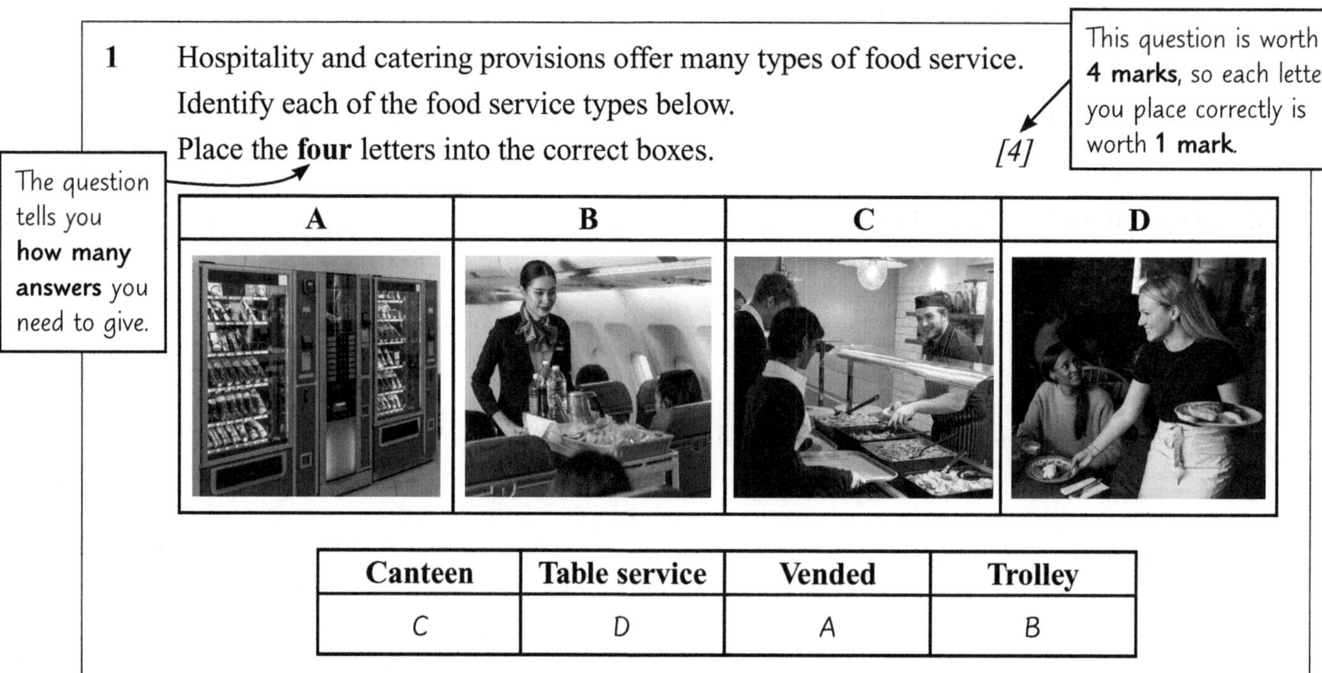

1 Hospitality and catering provisions offer many types of food service.
Identify each of the food service types below.
Place the **four** letters into the correct boxes. [4]

This question is worth **4 marks**, so each letter you place correctly is worth **1 mark**.

The question tells you **how many answers** you need to give.

A	B	C	D

Canteen	Table service	Vended	Trolley
C	D	A	B

'True or False...' questions are usually worth 4 marks

For '**True or False**' questions, you just need to **decide** if the statement given is true or false.

2 Tick (✓) the box next to each statement to show if it is **True** or **False**. [4]

	True	False
A freezer should be kept at -12 °C.		✓
A chef should not work in the kitchen if they are ill.	✓	
Frozen chicken breasts should be defrosted in the fridge.	✓	
Chefs should use a yellow chopping board for raw fish.		✓

Answering 'Explain' Questions

'**Explain**' questions are usually worth 4 marks. You can pick up a lot of marks in your exam from 4-mark questions, so it's really important that you know exactly how to answer them.

Make sure you explain each point you make

To answer a 4-mark '**Explain**' question, aim to make **four** points that are **well-explained**. This gives you the best chance of bagging **all four** available marks. Your points must be **relevant** to the context in the question. E.g. if the question is about catering in a residential establishment for older adults **don't** talk about the dietary needs of young children.

The examiner will use **descriptions** like in the table below to decide how many marks your answer gets:

Marks	Description
4	For a very good explanation of the topic in the question.
3	For a good explanation of the topic in the question.
2	For a basic explanation of the topic in the question.
1	For a limited explanation of the topic in the question. Response may be a list.
0	Response not creditworthy or not attempted.

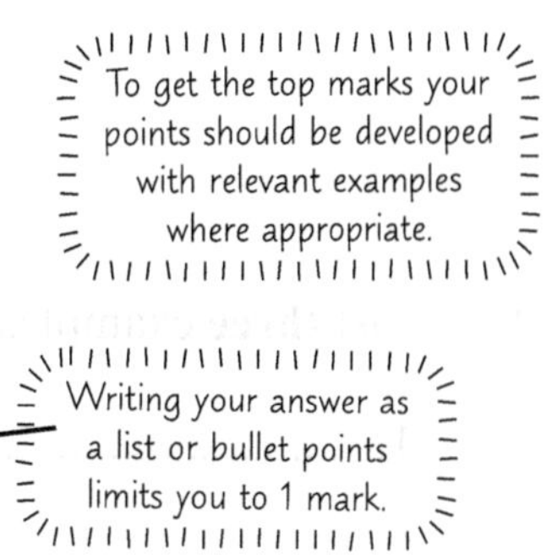

Here's an example of a 4-mark 'Explain...' question

3 Buffet style food service is popular in hotels which cater to families with young children. Explain the **benefits** of buffet style service to this type of customer. *[4]*

Buffet service is quicker so families will spend less time waiting in the restaurant which could give them more time to enjoy the hotel's facilities, such as the pool or play area.

Buffet service means a variety of foods can be tried, rather than customers having to commit to one choice. This means children, who can be fussy, will be more likely to find some food they like.

Buffet service allows customers to start eating as soon as they've visited the food counter instead of having to wait to be served. This is likely to be appreciated by families with impatient children.

A buffet service is less expensive to operate than table service as fewer waiting staff are required, so it is likely to be cheaper, which may be important for families that need to buy several meals.

This answer gets *4* mark(s) out of 4, because *four benefits have been identified. They are all benefits to the customer, not to the hotel, which is what the question asks for. They are also all relevant to the context of a hotel catering to families with children. Each point is developed with a well-written explanation.*

It's really important to link your points to the type of customer specified in the question. Don't just talk about the general benefits of buffets.

A **2-mark** 'Explain...' question may pop up in the exam. If it does, give two explained points.

Commercial and Non-Commercial Provision

1 Place the **four** hospitality and catering providers into the table below.

mobile food van   hostel   care home   factory canteen

Residential	Non-residential

[4]

2 List **three** examples of non-commercial hospitality and catering provision.

1. ....
2. ....
3. ....

[3]

3 Identify **one** type of establishment that fits each description.

(a) Offers private accommodation and breakfast.
Smaller than a hotel, often with communal areas. ....
[1]

(b) Offers made-to-order food.
Food is prepared quickly and often eaten elsewhere. ....
[1]

4 Name **three** leisure facilities that are often found in a hotel.

1. ....
2. ....
3. ....

[3]

Commercial and Non-Commercial Provision

5 Tick (✓) the box next to each statement to show if it is True or False.

	True	False
An aim of a coffee shop is usually to make a profit.		
A cruise ship is an example of commercial non-residential provision.		
Non-commercial establishments do not aim to make a profit.		

[3]

6 An amusement park focuses on providing entertainment as its main service.

(a) Give **two** ways that an amusement park may provide food and drink as an additional service.

1. ....

....

2. ....

....

[2]

(b) Name **one other** non-residential establishment that may offer food and drink as an additional service.

....

[1]

7 Teresa has been invited to attend a business conference at a local hotel.
Give **two** reasons why a hotel is an appropriate establishment to hold a business conference.

1. ....

....

2. ....

....

[2]

Exam Tip

Exam questions will give you the number of answers you need to write in **bold**. For command words like 'State', 'Name' or 'List', you'll get 1 mark for each correct answer you put down. If you know your stuff, they're easy marks.

Types of Food Service

1 List **three** types of table service.

1. ....

2. ....

3. ....

[3]

2 Give **one** benefit of family-style service.

....

....

[1]

3 A fast-food outlet offers counter service for customers eating in.
They also have a driver who delivers food directly to customers' homes.

(a) Give **one** benefit of counter service:

(i) for the customer.

....

....

[1]

(ii) for the establishment.

....

....

[1]

(b) Other than home delivery, state **one** type of personal service.

....

[1]

4 Give **two** reasons why a restaurant may choose to **not** use guéridon service.

1. ....

....

2. ....

....

[2]

Types of Food Service

5 Describe the similarities and differences between plate service and silver service.

....

....

....

....

....

....

....

....

[4]

6 Polly offers a cafeteria service in her coffee shop.
Outline the service a customer should expect in her shop.

....

....

....

....

[2]

7 Large wedding receptions often have a banquet.
Recommend a service style suitable for a banquet with lots of guests.
Give **two** reasons for your answer.

Choice of service style: ....

1. ....

....

2. ....

....

[3]

Exam Tip

Why not invent a memory aid to help you remember the different types of food service? Here's one I use for table service: Pandas Grab Short Bamboo First can jog your memory on Plate, Guéridon, Silver, Banquet and Family-Style.

Standards and Ratings

1 Tick (✓) the box next to each statement to show if it is True or False.

	True	False
Michelin stars are awarded based on the standard of service only.		
The highest number of Michelin stars is three.		
Michelin stars can be awarded to individual chefs.		

[3]

2 A restaurant has been downgraded from 3 AA rosettes to 1 AA rosette after a recent inspection. Outline **one** impact that this could have on the restaurant.

....

....

....

....

[2]

3 There are two hotels in the town of Whiteport.

The Red Drake 1-star hotel	The Blue Dragon 5-star hotel

Describe the differences in the facilities and service expected between the two hotels.

....

....

....

....

....

....

....

....

[4]

Employment Roles and Qualifications

1 List **two** housekeeping roles in a hospitality and catering establishment.

1. ....

2. ....

[2]

2 Felix is hiring a commis chef for his restaurant.
Suggest **three** relevant qualifications that a suitable candidate may hold.

1. ....

2. ....

3. ....

[3]

3 Place the **four** employment roles in the correct place in the table.

waiting staff kitchen porter pastry chef valet

Front of house	Back of house

[4]

4 Outline the responsibilities of a front of house manager.

....

....

....

....

[2]

Exam Tip

There are a lot of roles in the hospitality and catering industry — the 'front of house' roles are those that directly deal with customers. So these are the people you would see if you were a guest at the establishment.

Employment Roles and Qualifications

5 Look at the job advert on the right.

(a) Identify the role that is being advertised.

> *Management position available at local bistro.*
> *Responsibilities:*
> - *Promote our bistro using email.*
> - *Keep our website up to date.*

....

....

[1]

(b) Give **one** way that the advertised role could attract customers using email.

....

....

[1]

6 Give **two** benefits of doing a catering apprenticeship.

1. ....

....

2. ....

....

[2]

7 The hierarchy of a kitchen brigade is shown below. The most senior role is at the top.
Fill in the missing roles and **one** key responsibility of that role.

Role	**Key responsibility**
....	....
↓ Sous-chef	Oversees kitchen staff.
↓	....
↓ Commis chef	Helps other chefs with easier tasks.
↓ ...	

[4]

Employment Roles and Qualifications

8 Omar is applying to be the maître d'hôtel of a hotel restaurant.

(a) Give **three** responsibilities of a maître d'hôtel.

1. ....

2. ....

3. ....

[3]

(b) Give **two** personal skills and attributes that Omar will need to be successful in his role.

1. ....

2. ....

[2]

9 Outline **one** front of house role you might expect in a 5-star hotel, but not a 1-star hotel.

....

....

....

....

[2]

10 Describe the responsibilities of a food and beverage manager.

....

....

....

....

....

....

....

....

[4]

Exam Tip

The kitchen brigade sounds a bit like a superhero squad, but it's not that flashy — it's just the name for the framework of roles that help a kitchen run smoothly. You'll need to know about each role and what their responsibilities are.

Contracts and Working Hours

1 List **two** advantages for an employee of being employed on a full-time contract.

1. ....

....

2. ....

....

[2]

2 Sharon works for an event caterer on a temporary full-time contract.

(a) State what is meant by a temporary contract.

....

....

[1]

(b) Give **one** disadvantage for Sharon being on a temporary contract.

....

....

[1]

3 State **two** laws on working hours that apply to employees over 18.

1. ....

....

2. ....

....

[2]

4 Suggest a type of employment contract that would be suitable for a student in full-time education. Justify your answer.

Type of contract: ....

....

....

....

[2]

Pay and Benefits

1 Look at the social media post below.

The Windy Inn
18 Nov

We're hiring a part-time bartender to work 3 days a week.

- Salary of £18,000 — pay above National Minimum Wage
- 16.8 days' holiday entitlement a year

(a) State what is meant by the National Minimum Wage.

....

....

[1]

(b) Outline what is meant by a salary.

....

....

....

....

[2]

(c) Give **one** reason why someone may turn down this job in favour of a full-time bartender role.

....

....

[1]

2 Aaron is a 40-year-old waiter who has a full-time contract at a restaurant. Other than a salary and the benefits his employer must legally provide, identify **two** benefits that Aaron might receive.

1. ....

....

2. ....

....

[2]

Exam Tip

Remuneration is the fancy word that refers to the money an employee receives. Break it down as re - money - ration to help you remember. But don't forget — many employees receive other benefits that aren't money, like vouchers.

Costs, Profits and Economic Impact

1 Explain **three** types of cost for a hospitality and catering business.

1. ....

....

....

....

2. ....

....

....

....

3. ....

....

....

....

[6]

2 Aliyah calculates the cost of a full English breakfast in her café.

Cost of ingredients:	£3
Selling price:	£12

(a) State whether Aliyah makes a **positive** or **negative** gross profit on her dish. Justify your answer.

....

....

....

....

[2]

(b) Outline why VAT would be included in the price paid by customers for this dish.

....

....

....

....

[2]

Costs, Profits and Economic Impact

3 Outline **one** advantage of a strong economy for the hospitality and catering sector.

....

....

....

....

[2]

4 Bob owns a burger van. He make his burgers using local ingredients only.
He also offers high-end relishes that customers can add to their burger free of charge.
His food sales and total costs for the month are shown below.

Food Sales:	£5000
Total Costs:	£6000

(a) State whether Bob made a positive or negative net profit this month. Justify your answer.

....

....

....

....

[2]

(b) Give **four** actions that Bob could take to increase his net profit.

1. ....

....

2. ....

....

3. ....

....

4. ....

....

[4]

Exam Tip

The gross profit of a dish is the selling price minus the amount it costs to make (so the cost of the ingredients, but NOT the costs of the overheads and labour). However, the net profit of a business is different — it's the total sales minus all the costs (these include the cost of the ingredients AND the costs of the overheads and labour).

Environmental Impacts

1 Give **two** ways that a hospitality and catering business can be more energy efficient:

(a) in the kitchen

1. ....

....

2. ....

....

[2]

(b) in accommodation

1. ....

....

2. ....

....

[2]

2 Rachel owns a restaurant that specialises in Mediterranean cuisines.
She changes her menu regularly, depending on which seasonal foods are available.
Give **two** benefits of doing this.

1. ....

....

2. ....

....

[2]

3 Suggest **three** actions that a hospitality and catering business can take to reduce waste.

1. ....

....

2. ....

....

3. ....

....

[3]

The Impact of Technology

1 Kento owns a popular café. He only accepts cashless payments.

(a) Outline **one** reason why he may prefer to take cashless payments only.

....

....

....

....

[2]

(b) List **two** ways customers can make cashless payments.

1. ....

2. ....

[2]

2 Explain how technology can benefit a customer staying at a hotel.

....

....

....

....

....

....

....

....

[4]

3 Outline **one** way that record-keeping technology can make a hospitality and catering business more efficient.

....

....

....

....

[2]

Exam Tip

You might be asked about the impact of technology on a customer or on a business (or both in long questions) — make sure your answer matches what's required by the question, or you might throw away some marks.

The Impact of Media

1 Outline **one** way that a hospitality and catering business can use media to stand out from their competitors.

....

....

....

....

[2]

2 Raj has opened up a dessert parlour. He uses social media to promote the business.
Give **one** advantage and **one** disadvantage of using social media as his **only** form of promotion.

Advantage: ....

....

Disadvantage: ....

....

[2]

3 Office Elves is a business that specialises in catering for corporate Christmas parties.
Outline how Office Elves could promote their business using:

(a) printed media

....

....

....

....

[2]

(b) broadcast media

....

....

....

....

[2]

Operational Requirements

1 List **three** front of house areas of a hospitality and catering business.

1. ....

2. ....

3. ....

[3]

2 Fill in the missing stages in the **workflow** for a kitchen in a hospitality and catering business.

Goods are delivered by suppliers. → .... → Goods are put in the correct place in the storage area. → Food is removed from storage area. → .... → Food is plated up.

[2]

3 Receptionists are often the first point of contact for customers of a residential business.

(a) Identify **two** main responsibilities of receptionists when checking customers in.

1. ....

2. ....

[2]

(b) Explain why good communication between reception and housekeeping is essential.

....

....

....

....

....

....

....

....

[4]

Operational Requirements

4 Describe the similarities and differences between the **front of house layout** of a **table service** restaurant and that of a **counter service** restaurant.

[4]

5 Outline how **one** aspect of a commercial kitchen layout improves the safety of:

(a) kitchen staff

[2]

(b) customers with allergies

[2]

6 Give **two** reasons why it is important for a café to provide dedicated areas for staff.

1.

2.

[2]

Exam Tip

Remember, to ace 'Explain' questions (like question 3b), each point you give must have a linked explanation. Check how many marks the question is worth too — for a 4-mark 'Explain' question you should aim to make four points.

Equipment, Materials and Dress Code

1 For each task below, identify **one** large scale piece of equipment used in a commercial kitchen. State how it improves efficiency.

Task: Food storage

Piece of equipment: ....

How it improves efficiency: ....

....

Tasks: Food preparation

Piece of equipment: ....

How it improves efficiency: ....

....

Tasks: Cleaning dishes and utensils

Piece of equipment: ....

How it improves efficiency: ....

....

[6]

2 Place the **four** pieces of equipment into the table below according to their use.

spatula chopping board baking tray measuring jug

Preparation	Cooking

[4]

3 Name **three** pieces of safety equipment that are required in a commercial kitchen.

1. ....
2. ....
3. ....

[3]

Equipment, Materials and Dress Code

4 Outline **one** advantage for a hospitality and catering business of buying high-quality equipment.

....

....

....

....

[2]

5 Dress codes for kitchen staff are often related to health and safety.
Label the items shown in the photograph below and describe the purpose of each.

Item: ....

Purpose: ....

....

....

....

....

Item: ....

Purpose: ....

....

....

....

....

Item: ....

Purpose: ....

....

[6]

6 Explain why front of house staff are often required to follow rules about their appearance.

....

....

....

....

....

....

....

[4]

Exam Tip

Make sure you know the names of they key pieces of equipment used in commercial kitchens — their purpose is usually to make everything as efficient as possible. Safety is critical too — what, with all the flames, chopping and hot liquids.

Administration and Documentation

1 Tick (✓) the box next to each statement to show if it is True or False.

	True	False
Only large businesses need to report major injuries to HSE.		
Businesses with more than 10 employees must keep records of all injuries.		

[2]

2 Outline **one** advantage of a computerised stock control system over a manual system.

....

....

....

....

[2]

3 Information from the lids of two yoghurt containers is shown on the right. Outline how they should be stored when using a FIFO system.

Delivered on 28th February	USE BY 10 MAR
Delivered on 7th March	**USE BY 18 MAR**

....

....

....

....

[2]

4 Catering businesses should keep records of deliveries.
Explain why deliveries should be carefully checked when they arrive.

....

....

....

....

....

....

....

....

[4]

Meeting Customer Needs

1 Residential hospitality and catering establishments must meet a range of different needs.

(a) Outline **one** way that establishments can meet the needs of **local residents**.

....

....

....

....

[2]

(b) Describe the similarities and differences between the typical needs of **leisure** and **business** guests.

....

....

....

....

....

....

....

[4]

2 Part of a letter of complaint to a restaurant is shown below.

> *The menu stated that the Chicken Kiev was made from a whole chicken breast, but it was made of processed chicken.*
>
> *My husband had ordered the same meal as me but was given twice as many chips. I was told that this was because he was a man and I wasn't.*

Identify which **two** of the following sets of laws are relevant in this situation.
Give a reason for each choice.

Health and Safety at Work Act   Consumer Rights Act   Equality Act   Food Safety

Laws: ....

Reasons: ....

....

Laws: ....

Reasons: ....

....

[4]

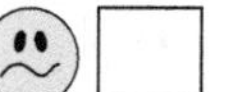

Meeting Customer Needs

3 Explain how hospitality and catering businesses could adapt to meet the needs of guests with disabilities.

....

....

....

....

....

....

....

[4]

4 At the Four-Legged Flamingo restaurant, a guest recently had an allergic reaction to peanuts. They weren't warned that the dish they'd ordered contained peanuts.

Recommend **two** actions the restaurant could take to reduce the risk of this happening again.

Recommendation 1: ....

....

....

Recommendation 2: ....

....

....

[4]

5 Explain why meeting customer needs would benefit a hospitality and catering provider.

....

....

....

....

....

....

....

[4]

Exam Tip

When you're asked about the benefits of something, make sure you talk about the benefits for the correct group of people or business. For example, for question 5 above, prattling on about benefits for customers will get you a zero.

Customer Expectations

1 Describe the similarities and differences between the likely expectations of a guest at an expensive luxury hotel and a guest at a budget guest house.

....

....

....

....

....

....

....

....

[4]

2 A restaurant advertises itself as environmentally-friendly.
State **three** likely expectation of guests who visit this restaurant.

1. ....

2. ....

3. ....

[3]

3 Outline **one** way that social media can influence the expectations of hotel guests.

....

....

....

....

[2]

4 Outline why hospitality and catering providers should keep up to date with changing trends.

....

....

....

....

[2]

Customer Demographics

1 A new hotel is being built next to a theme park.

(a) Suggest **one** group of customers that the hotel should target.

....

[1]

(b) Outline **two** facilities or services the hotel could offer to appeal to your suggested target market.

1. ....

....

....

2. ....

....

....

[4]

2 The graph below shows the types of catering establishments in Little Snodsworth.

An entrepreneur is considering setting up a catering establishment in Little Snodsworth.

(a) Identify the type of establishment that would have the least competition.

....

[1]

(b) Suggest a target market for the type of establishment you have identified in part (a).
Give **one** reason for your answer.

Target market: ....

Reason: ....

....

[2]

Exam Tip

Examiners love a graph — and customer demographics is a handy way to get one into the exam paper. If you're presented with one, look carefully at the information it gives you — you'll be expected to base your answer on it.

Health and Safety Laws

1 A hotel provides disposable gloves and safety glasses for the cleaning staff it employs. This is required by the Personal Protective Equipment at Work Regulations (1992).

(a) Other than providing these items, give **two** responsibilities of the hotel as an employer under these regulations.

1. ....

....

2. ....

....

[2]

(b) Give **one** responsibility of the cleaning staff under these regulations.

....

....

[1]

2 The Manual Handling Operations Regulations must be followed by employers and employees.

(a) Outline the **aim** of the Manual Handling Operations Regulations.

....

....

....

....

[2]

(b) A employee has been asked to move a heavy object in a hospitality and catering establishment. Give **one** thing the employee should do at each stage of the process in the table below.

Stage	What employee must do
Assess the situation	....
Lift the object	....
Carry the object	....

[3]

Health and Safety Laws

3 Outline what is required of **employers** by RIDDOR.

....

....

....

....

[2]

4 State **three** responsibilities of **employees** under the Health and Safety at Work Act.

1. ....
2. ....
3. ....

[3]

5 A business uses a cleaning chemical which shows the symbol on the right.

(a) Outline **one** type of document that the business must complete for this product.

....

....

....

....

[2]

(b) Other than completing a document, describe the responsibilities of **employers** relating to the use of this chemical.

....

....

....

....

....

....

....

[4]

Exam Tip

There are five sets of regulations you need to know about. They're all a mouthful so are often referred to by their initial letters — HASAWA, RIDDOR, COSHH, MHOR and PPER. Employers and employees have different responsibilities under each set of regulations — so double-check which group of people the question is asking about.

Accident Forms and Risk Assessments

1 A commis chef suffered a broken wrist when they slipped on wet floor next to the sink.

(a) Give **two** ways that this hazard could have been reduced.

1. ....

....

2. ....

....

[2]

(b) Give **one** reason why an accident form must be completed after this incident.

....

....

[1]

2 Risk assessments need to consider the risks to everyone.

(a) Identify **three** hazards which may cause harm to **customers** at a restaurant.
For each hazard, give **one** control measure.

	Hazard	Control measure
1.	....	....
2.	....	....
3	....	....

[6]

(b) Employers should assess the **level of risk** for each hazard. State what is meant by this.

....

....

[1]

Hazard Analysis and Critical Control Points

1 There are three main types of food hazard.

(a) Give **one** example of a **physical** food hazard.

....

[1]

(b) Name the **two** other main types of food hazard.

1. ....

2. ....

[2]

2 For each control point below, state the type of hazard controlled and how the risk is reduced.

(a) Servers must wear a hair net.

Type of hazard: ....

How risk is reduced: ....

[2]

(b) Food should be cooked to above 75 °C.

Type of hazard: ....

How risk is reduced: ....

[2]

(c) Cover food when cleaning work surfaces.

Type of hazard: ....

How risk is reduced: ....

[2]

3 Complete the extract from a HACCP table below.

Stage	Hazard	Control point
Storing food	....	....

[2]

Exam Tip

Exam questions will often ask you to complete a HACCP table. Learn at least two ways that something nasty could contaminate food at each stage — from obtaining the ingredients, to handing the finished dish to the customer.

Food-Induced Ill-Health

1 A food intolerance can cause ill-health.

(a) Outline what is meant by a food intolerance.

....

....

....

....

[2]

(b) Other than a food intolerance, give **two** causes of food-induced ill-health.

1. ....

2. ....

[2]

2 Place the **four** allergens into the correct place in the table.

molluscs ginger soya mustard

Common allergen	Not a common allergen

[4]

3 For each food intolerance below, name **one** food it is commonly found in.

(a) lactose

....

[1]

(b) gluten

....

[1]

(c) aspartame

....

[1]

Exam Tip

Outline questions (like Q1a), are usually worth 2 marks. A very brief description covering the topic will net you 1 mark, but you'll need to add more depth to your answer (to show you really know your stuff) to get both of the marks.

Food-Induced Ill-Health

4 Food-induced ill-health can result in visible symptoms and non-visible symptoms.

(a) Give **two** visible symptoms of food-induced ill-health.

1. ....

2. ....

[2]

(b) Give **two** non-visible symptoms of food-induced ill-health.

1. ....

2. ....

[2]

5 Name **one** food source where the following bacteria can be found.

(a) *E.coli*

....

[1]

(b) *Campylobacter*

....

[1]

(c) *Listeria*

....

[1]

6 Lee has a gluten intolerance. He experiences symptoms after eating a dish at a café.
List **two** symptoms he may experience.

1. ....

2. ....

[2]

7 Outline what is meant by anaphylaxis.

....

....

....

....

[2]

Food-Induced Ill-Health

8 Erika cooks a large batch of rice. She leaves the cooked rice on the counter overnight, then stores it in the refrigerator.
Outline why the rice is a potential risk even if she reheats it.

[2]

9 Outline **one** way a dish could be contaminated with *Clostridium perfringens*.

[2]

10 Bea's B&B serves eggs Benedict with smoked salmon at breakfast.
The ingredients used in the dish are shown below.

egg, vinegar, English muffin (bread), butter, smoked salmon, chives, bottled lemon juice

(a) Identify **two** common allergens in this dish.

1.
2.

[2]

(b) Name **one** example of bacteria that could be present in the dish if Bea doesn't maintain strict food hygiene. Explain your answer.

Bacteria:

[2]

Exam Tip

There are different ways food can cause ill-health. Allergies and intolerances are two of the biggies (allergies can be life-threatening, but not intolerances). Then you've got contamination from bacteria, mould, chemicals, fingernails...

Preventing Food-Induced Ill-Health

1 Ali has booked a meal at a local restaurant. He has a severe allergy to nuts.
Outline **one** action you would expect the restaurant to take to ensure his safety.

....

....

....

....
[2]

2 The head chef at the King's Head pub has ordered some cooked prawns.
The prawns were refrigerated during delivery and their temperature was checked on arrival.

Temperature of prawns

7 °C

Outline what action the head chef should take with the delivery.

....

....

....

....
[2]

3 Give **four** ways of reducing cross-contamination from raw foods
to ready-to-eat foods in a commercial kitchen.

1. ....

....

2. ....

....

3. ....

....

4. ....

....
[4]

Preventing Food-Induced Ill-Health

4 Give the correct temperature control required when:

(a) hot-holding buffet food

....

....

[1]

(b) freezing leftovers

....

....

[1]

5 List **two** measures a kitchen assistant should take to prevent cross-contamination.

1. ....

....

2. ....

....

[2]

6 Describe the control measures a hospitality and catering establishment may take to help prevent the physical contamination of food.

....

....

....

....

....

....

....

....

[4]

Exam Tip

Temperature control is super important for a catering business — you should commit to memory the key temperatures for freezing, chilling and cooking or reheating food. You might have to apply this knowledge to a food safety context.

Catering and the Law

1 All catering establishments are expected to follow food safety laws.

(a) Give **two** responsibilities of catering establishments under the Food Safety Act (1990).

1. ....

....

2. ....

....

[2]

(b) Name **one** other set of laws that aims to ensure food is handled safely in catering establishments.

....

[1]

2 Rahul often buys ready-made sauces and condiments to use in his café.
The labels show useful information required by law.

(a) Justify why each of these pieces of information is useful to customers or Rahul.

(i) common allergens highlighted in bold

....

....

....

....

[2]

(ii) how to store the product

....

....

....

....

[2]

(b) List **four** other pieces of information that would be shown on the label of a pre-packaged food.

1. ....
2. ....
3. ....
4. ....

[4]

Role of the EHO

1 An EHO is carrying out an inspection of a hospitality and catering establishment.

(a) Outline the key responsibilities of an EHO.

....

....

....

....

[2]

(b) Give **two** reasons why an EHO may be inspecting an establishment.

1. ....

2. ....

[2]

(c) Give **three** specific checks an EHO may carry out during an inspection.

1. ....

....

2. ....

....

3. ....

....

[3]

2 Give **three** actions an EHO can take if a catering business performs poorly during an inspection.

1. ....

....

2. ....

....

3. ....

....

[3]

Exam Tip

The role of the EHO can be a popular 6- or 8-mark exam question since there's a fair bit to talk about (there's an example on p.46). It can help to plan out your answer first using bullets before you write a more detailed response. Think about what an EHO checks, how they gather evidence and the actions they may take following a poor inspection.

Extended-Answer Questions

Extended-response questions are worth a juicy **6-8 marks**, so it's vital you know how to answer them.

Here's an example of a 6-mark 'Describe...' question

1 The Lily Pad Children's Den and Café has recently appointed more waiting staff due to an increased number of customers. The Lily Pad offers both a children's menu and an adult's menu to cater for its target customers (toddlers and their parents).

Describe the skills and personal qualities needed by the waiting staff.
Link your answer to the **success** of the business. *[6]*

The **mark scheme** for this type of question will contain lists of things that an answer may include. For example:

Skills:

- Food hygiene
- First aid
- Prioritisation
- Clear handwriting
- Numeracy
- ICT skills
- Verbal communication
- Listening
- Problem solving

Personal qualities:

- Cheerful — e.g. when welcoming customers
- Supportive — able to work in a team
- Calm — able to work under pressure
- Confident — able to make decisions
- Efficient — able to get lots of tasks done quickly
- Patient — when dealing with customers
- Adaptable — able to help out in other areas
- Conscientious — carries out tasks thoroughly
- Trustworthy — e.g. when dealing with money

You aren't limited to these points — examiners will be told to 'credit any other valid response'.

When it comes to deciding **how many marks** your answer is worth, the examiner will be guided by descriptions of different **bands**. This table sums up the features that make an answer fit into each band:

Band	Description
3	**Award 5-6 marks** For a very good answer with a developed understanding of a wide range of skills and personal qualities needed by waiting staff and their impacts on the success of the business. A range of relevant areas are covered.
2	**Award 3-4 marks** For a good answer where candidates have shown a good understanding of a range of skills and personal qualities needed by waiting staff and their impacts on the success of the business.
1	**Award 1-2 marks** For a basic answer where candidates have shown limited understanding of the skills and personal qualities needed by waiting staff and their impacts on the success of the business. Answer may resemble a list.
	0 Response not creditworthy or not attempted.

Writing your answer as a list or bullet points limits you to Band 1, or a maximum of 2 marks, no matter how many points you make.

There are some **sample answers** to this question on the next page.

Extended-Answer Questions

Compare these two sample answers

Below are two answers to the question on the previous page. Look at the explanation of how many marks each would get. Compare this to the mark scheme on the previous page.

Answer 1

Waiting staff at the Lily Pad would need to be cheerful.

The staff would need to know how to use the till.

The staff would have to be friendly and patient with children.

The answer gets *2* mark(s) out of 6, because *it is a basic answer that could be a list so it would be in Band 1. There is no explanation as to why the staff should be cheerful, or be friendly and patient with children. There is also no reason given for why using the till is essential to their role as waiting staff or to the success of the business.*

Answer 2

Waiting staff at the Lily Pad should have food hygiene skills as they are serving food to the public. This would help them keep people with food allergies safe and avoid damage to the Lily Pad's reputation. Waiting staff would also need good listening skills so that they can take orders from customers correctly and have good written communication skills so that they can communicate the orders accurately to the kitchen. If an EPOS system is used for taking orders, ICT skills would be important. Not being able to take orders accurately would lead to food wastage, which would damage the Lily Pad's profits as meals would need to be remade. Customers sometimes can't decide what they want, especially children, so staff would need to be patient. Also, the Lily Pad may sometimes be busy, so staff would need to be calm so they could continue providing a good service to customers. If the staff aren't patient or calm, customers are likely to write negative reviews on social media, which may put people off visiting. A first aid qualification would be useful as children may hurt themselves when playing. If parents feel the Lily Pad is a safe place for their children, they will return and recommend it to their friends.

This answer gets *6* mark(s) out of 6, because *a wide range of skills and qualities are identified. Each of them is linked to an explanation or an example, e.g. the need for good listening skills is linked to taking orders accurately. Awareness of the impacts of the skills or qualities on the success of the business is also shown, e.g. wasting food or getting negative reviews would damage profits.*

Extended-Answer Questions

Here's an example of an 8-mark 'Discuss...' question

2 The Highwayman is a new bistro serving breakfast, lunch and evening meals to local residents and passing tourists. Samir is applying for a the position of head chef at The Highwayman.
Discuss the responsibilities of the head chef at The Highwayman. *[8]*

The **mark scheme** for this type of question will list **examples** of things which answers could include. Like for the question on page 39, there will also be descriptions of each **band** to help the examiner decide how many marks to award. As this question has 8-marks available, there are **four bands**:

Band	Description
4	**Award 7-8 marks** An excellent response demonstrating a wide range of accurate knowledge. Relevant responsibilities are given with a good level of detail. There is precise use of terminology.
3	**Award 5-6 marks** A very good response demonstrating accurate knowledge. Some appropriate responsibilities are given, with a good level of detail. There is precise use of terminology.
2	**Award 3-4 marks** A good response demonstrating some knowledge. There is generally precise use of appropriate terminology.
1	**Award 1-2 marks** A basic response demonstrating limited knowledge. A few responsibilities are given, possibly as bullet points or a list. There is some use of appropriate terminology.
	0 Response not creditworthy or not attempted.

As you saw on page 39, writing your answer as a list or bullet points will limit you to Band 1. Here that means a maximum of 2 marks.

Now for two sample answers

Below is an answer to the question above with an explanation of how many marks it would get. There's a second sample answer on the next page.

Answer 1

The head chef at The Highwayman will:
- *Plan the menu.*
- *Order ingredients.*
- *Hire and train staff.*
- *Manage the kitchen brigade.*

This answer gets *2* mark(s) out of 8, because *it shows a basic understanding of the responsibilities of a head chef by using a few examples. The points are accurate, but they lack detail. The answer is given as bullet points so it's worth a maximum of 2 marks.*

Extended-Answer Questions

Now it's your turn to be the examiner. Read Answer 2 below, then work out which description from the mark scheme fits this sample answer best to find the mark you think it deserves.

Answer 2

In the exam, you'd be given more lines than this for your answer.

The head chef is responsible for the day-to-day running of the kitchen, for example recruiting staff and organising rotas and shifts. They must supervise the kitchen brigade to make sure that dishes are made to a high standard, e.g. that they are garnished correctly. The head chef will also need to train staff and support their development, e.g. make sure a commis chef has the opportunity to improve their skills. They must also motivate the kitchen brigade so that the morale of the team is high enough to deliver the best quality food every time. The head chef is also responsible for health and safety in the kitchen, e.g. making sure that staff only use equipment they've been trained to use. The head chef is responsible for food safety too, so must make sure staff follow guidelines to avoid cross contamination and ensure that allergens are correctly labelled. The head chef will also plan menu changes, e.g. meals for a new winter menu, and keeps track of the finances, e.g. makes sure a budget is stuck to and they get the best price for ingredients from suppliers.

I would give this answer ...... mark(s) out of 8, because ....

....

....

....

....

Now compare what you wrote to our mark and reasoning on page 73.

Watch out for 'Evaluate...' questions

'**Evaluate**' questions are a bit like '**Discuss**' questions but require you to include a **conclusion**. To achieve the **highest marks** in 'Evaluate' questions, you must:

- Provide a detailed, sensible conclusion.
- Back your conclusion up with reasoning or evidence.

The mark scheme for 'Evaluate' questions will be similar to the one on page 41.

Here's an example of an 8-mark 'Evaluate...' question

3 Technology is playing an increasingly large role in the running of a hotel.
Evaluate the positive and negative impacts for hotels of using technology. *[8]*

There's a **sample answer** to this question on the next page.

Extended-Answer Questions

A **range** of points have been made, which all have a good level of **detail**.

Specific, appropriate **advantages** and **disadvantages** create a **balanced** argument.

It's **really clear** to the examiner that the **conclusion** starts here.

The points made above have been used to **support** the conclusion.

A positive impact of technology for hotels is that it decreases the workload of reception, e.g. customers can self check-in at any time. This means fewer reception staff are needed, so the costs for the hotel are reduced. EPOS systems that can keep track of guest spending in different areas of the hotel, such as the restaurant or the spa are another positive. A final bill can be generated, which reduces the risk of missing off items which would reduce profits. Another positive are apps that can allow customers to make dinner reservations and order room service, so reception staff do not need to send messages to the restaurant. Information, such as breakfast times or entertainment schedules, can also be displayed in an app, meaning staff don't need to print posters or leaflets and update them if details change. This reduces printing costs as well as labour costs.

A negative impact of technology for hotels is that they may lose customers who struggle to use technology such as touchscreens, or who don't own a smartphone. Customers may also miss dealing with a member of staff on the front desk, or find it difficult to explain their particular needs using a computer. Another negative is that technical problems, e.g. with an app, can lead to poor customer service and damage the hotel's reputation.

In conclusion, I think the positive impact of reduced costs for the hotel outweighs the lost income from the small number of customers who decide not to stay at the hotel due to the use of technology. There will however need to be an offline system in place in case of technical problems, and to allow customers without a smartphone to access the services.

This answer would get **8 marks** out of 8 for the reasons given in the boxes on the left.

Top Tips for answering 6-8 mark questions

1. **Use the context.**
   Clearly link your answer to the context of the question, and keep it relevant to the specific establishment, job role, food service, etc.
2. **Consider different factors that apply.**
   Identify the most important points that are relevant to the context. For 'Evaluate' questions, weigh up both the positives and negatives, etc.
3. **Think about how your points relate to each other.**
   Your answer should make it clear how each of your points link together. Try to give examples.
4. **Write in full sentences and use key terminology.**
   You get marks for a well developed answer, so don't just use lists or bullet points. Use proper terminology when you can, but only if you're sure what the word means.
5. **Give a conclusion.**
   Finish off with a conclusion (if relevant), supported by the points you've provided.

Mixed Questions 1 — Yewbrook Care Home

1 Yewbrook Care Home provides accommodation and meals for its elderly residents. The care home chef has recently added a new chicken dish to the menu so the Hazard Analysis and Critical Control Points (HACCP) folder must be reviewed.

(a) Complete the Hazard and Control Point columns of the HACCP tables below.
Suggest **one** hazard and **one** control point for the **storage and preparation** of raw chicken.

Stage	Hazard	Control point
(i) Storage		
(ii) Preparation		

[4]

Suggest **one** hazard and **one** control point for **cooking and serving** the chicken dish.

Stage	Hazard	Control point
(iii) Cooking		
(iv) Serving		

[4]

Mixed Questions 1 — Yewbrook Care Home

(b) (i) Name **two** types of food poisoning bacteria found in raw chicken.

Bacteria 1: ....

Bacteria 2: ....

[2]

(ii) For **one** bacteria named in part (i), state **one** visible and **one** non-visible symptom.

Bacteria: ....

Visible symptom:

....

Non-visible symptom:

....

[2]

Food poisoning can be very dangerous for the elderly, so it's extremely important that the kitchen brigade at Yewbrook Care Home avoid contaminating food with bacteria.

(c) (i) Describe **two** ways that food such as salads can be contaminated with ***Staphylococcus aureus*** while they are being prepared.

(ii) For each, give **one** way that the risk can be controlled.

	Contamination hazard	How to control the risk
1.		
2.		

[4]

Exam Tip

You need to know about 7 types of bacteria that can cause food poisoning. For each one, make sure you memorise both visible and non-visible symptoms. Revise which types of high-risk food each bacteria is commonly found in too.

Mixed Questions 1 — Yewbrook Care Home

Like all hospitality and catering establishments, the care home is inspected regularly by an EHO.

(d) Discuss the role of an Environmental Health Officer (EHO) during and after an inspection.

....

....

....

....

....

....

....

....

....

....

....

....

....

....

....

....

[8]

Following the inspection, Yewbrook Care Home receives a Food Hygiene Rating of 2.

(e) Describe how this could affect the business.

....

....

....

....

....

....

....

....

[4]

Mixed Questions 2 — The Ramsden Hotel

2 The Ramsden Hotel facilities include a golf course, swimming pool, gym, spa, two restaurants and a small café. It allows local residents to pay to use the facilities.

The hotel also has three large conference rooms and a banqueting suite that are available to hire. There are 320 rooms in the hotel and 20 of these are accessible rooms located on the ground floor.

(a) Suggest **four** ways that The Ramsden Hotel might meet the needs of the following types of customer.

(i) Local families with children.

1. ....

....

2. ....

....

3. ....

....

4. ....

....

[4]

(ii) Local retired couples.

1. ....

....

2. ....

....

3. ....

....

4. ....

....

[4]

Exam Tip

Don't forget to take note of the number in **bold** that appears in a question. It tells you how many answers you'll need to give. On this page it's pretty hard to miss because each set of dotted lines is split up into 4 clear sets of two lines, but it might not look exactly like this in the exam, so keep an eye out to make sure you don't miss the bold numbers.

Mixed Questions 2 — The Ramsden Hotel

(iii) People visiting the area on business.

1. ....

....

2. ....

....

3. ....

....

4. ....

....

[4]

Abeni is the events manager at The Ramsden Hotel. Her role involves making sure that each event is a success and that clients are satisfied.

(b) Recommend **three** ways that Abeni could ensure that an event at which food is being served meets the client's needs.

1.

....

....

....

....

2.

....

....

....

....

3.

....

....

....

....

[6]

Mixed Questions 2 — The Ramsden Hotel

The Ramsden Hotel are hosting the local school's Year 11 prom. The school have surveyed students about the food they would prefer and have made a list of requirements. The following list has been given to Abeni.

Requirements:

- A good variety of hot and cold food options.
- Food to suit a mixture of dietary requirements including vegetarian, vegan and meat options that don't include pork.
- Food to cater for three students with a gluten intolerance and two other students with a nut allergy.
- Food service that doesn't take too long as the event is quite short and students want time to dance and socialise.
- The costs should be as low as possible so that ticket prices can be affordable for all.

Using information from the list of requirements:

(c) (i) Recommend **one** suitable type of food service for the prom based on the requirements.

....

[1]

(ii) Justify your choice of food service.

....

....

....

....

....

....

....

....

[4]

Exam Tip

If there's a chunk of information in a question (e.g. the list of requirements above) it'll be there for a reason. Read it carefully and use it to make your answer specific to the question (e.g. mention the cost requirement for the prom food).

Mixed Questions 2 — The Ramsden Hotel

All new staff at The Ramsden Hotel complete fire safety training when they start. During a busy Sunday lunch service the fire alarm sounds. Staff are not aware of any planned fire drills. There are several wheelchair users in the restaurant, which is located on the first floor.

(d) (i) Describe what the restaurant staff should do in this situation.

[8]

The fire alarm was set off by a small fire in another part of the hotel.

(ii) Outline what action should be taken after the fire.
Include the name of the relevant law in your answer.

[2]

Mixed Questions 3 — The Forge

3 The Forge is a high-end restaurant located in an affluent rural town. They have recently employed a new section chef (chef de partie) for the vegetable station.

(a) Describe the job role of the vegetable chef.

....

....

....

....

....

....

....

....

[4]

Teamwork is important in any kitchen brigade.

(b) Discuss the importance of teamwork to the continued success of a restaurant.

....

....

....

....

....

....

....

....

....

....

....

....

[6]

Exam Tip

If a question starts with 'Discuss' your answer shouldn't just describe something. Discuss questions are all about examining something in detail and taking into account different ideas, so remember this as you're writing your answer.

Mixed Questions 3 — The Forge

Members of staff at The Forge are employed on several different types of contract.
The new vegetable chef has been employed on a permanent full-time contract.

(c) (i) Discuss the benefits of this type of working contract for the **vegetable chef**.

....

....

....

....

....

....

....

....

....

....

....

....

[6]

(ii) Discuss the benefits of this type of working contract for the **restaurant owner**.

....

....

....

....

....

....

....

....

....

....

....

....

[6]

Mixed Questions 3 — The Forge

An AA Rosette is awarded to restaurants offering excellent quality food.
The Forge currently holds two AA rosettes.

(d) Discuss the benefits this award might have for the business.

....

....

....

....

....

....

....

....

....

....

....

....

[6]

An AA Rosette is one example of an award for food service that a hospitality and catering establishment can be given.

(e) Outline **two** other awards that an establishment can be given.

1. ....

....

2. ....

....

[4]

Exam Tip

AA Rosettes have been around since the 1950s and are a pretty good sign that a restaurant or hotel offers really high quality food, definitely not your standard pub grub. Restaurants can achieve between one and five Rosettes, but not many are awarded five. Those with five Rosettes are up there with the very best restaurants in the world.

Mixed Questions 4 — Running Rhino Bakery

4 Running Rhino Bakery has recently renovated its restaurant kitchen.

(a) Consider the new kitchen layout below.

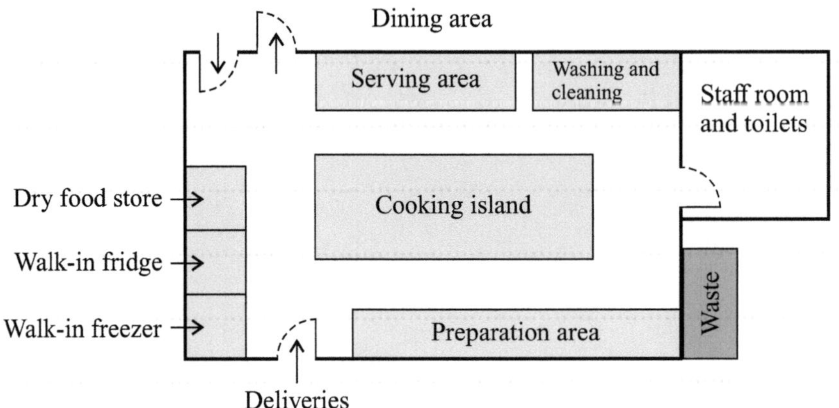

Describe the benefits that this layout will have on the following:

(i) food safety

....

....

....

....

....

....

....

....

[4]

(ii) health and safety of staff

....

....

....

....

....

....

....

....

[4]

Mixed Questions 4 — Running Rhino Bakery

Running Rhino Bakery is known for its dessert menu and afternoon teas and has become popular due to social media posts and recommendations. To keep up with the demand, the manager would like to increase the amount of food he can bake each day through the use of large-scale equipment.

(b) Recommend **two large scale** pieces of equipment the manager could purchase. Justify each of your choices.

Piece of equipment 1:

....

Justification:

....

....

....

....

Piece of equipment 2:

....

Justification:

....

....

....

....

[6]

(c) Outline **one** way that large scale equipment could reduce the bakery's costs.

....

....

....

....

[2]

Exam Tip

Written something stupid in the exam that you don't want the examiner to mark? Draw a neat, straight line through it (a bit like this: ~~walk-out freezer~~) to show that it is something that you don't want them to ~~mwrk~~ mark. Phew.

Mixed Questions 5 — Dunes Caravan Park

5 Steven is a commis chef working at Dunes Caravan Park over the busy summer season. He is 18 years old and started his employment in May 2023. He has recently been injured in an accident at work. Details of the accident are given in the accident form shown below.

Accident Form	
Date and time of accident	15/06/2023 10:17 am
Name of injured person(s)	Steven Smith
Accident and injury details	Whilst operating the meat slicer, Steven cut his finger deeply. Steven had been asked to cover the meat preparation station due to staff sickness. He was not trained in using the meat slicer.
Action taken	First aider (head chef) applied pressure and a dressing, but the bleeding didn't stop. Steven was then taken to A&E by the restaurant manager.

(a) Assess who was at fault. Justify your answer.

....

....

....

....

....

....

....

....

[4]

(b) Recommend **four** ways that similar accidents could be avoided in the future.

1. ....

....

2. ....

....

3. ....

....

4. ....

....

[4]

Mixed Questions 5 — Dunes Caravan Park

Following the accident a new risk assessment is carried out for the meat slicer.

(c) Complete the risk assessment form below by giving **four** control measures.

Risk Assessment		
Assessment carried out by: Tamsin Reed	**Date of Assessment**: 17/06/23	**Next review**: 17/06/24
Hazard: Operating Meat Slicer	**Risk**: Staff operating machine may suffer cuts, severed fingers, electrocution.	**Control measures required**: 1. .... 2. .... 3. .... 4. ....
	Risk level: High	**Who will monitor?** Manager and senior chefs

[4]

The layout of the kitchen is being changed to improve its efficiency. This involves staff moving the meat slicer, which weighs 22 kg, to a new position in the kitchen.

(d) Outline how the caravan park should prepare staff involved in moving the heavy meat slicer.

....

....

....

....

[2]

Exam Tip

Accident forms (like the one shown on the previous page) have to be completed whenever there's an accident in a workplace with more than 10 employees. The way they look can vary a bit, but they all record the accident details.

Mixed Questions 6 — Cactus Summer Camp

6 Cactus Summer Camp provides breakfast and lunch for 70 children at their on-site canteen. Each child was surveyed about their dietary needs before attending the camp.

(a) Analyse the survey results below and discuss how the canteen staff can meet the dietary and nutritional requirements of the children.

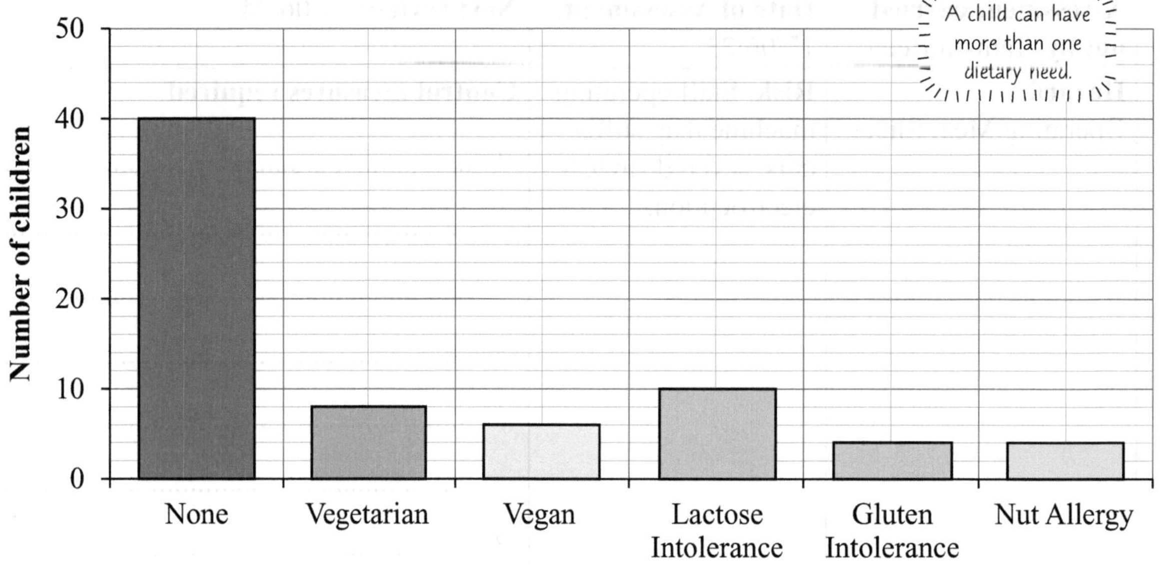

....

....

....

....

....

....

....

....

....

....

....

....

....

....

....

....

[8]

Mixed Questions 6 — Cactus Summer Camp

Finlay had a severe allergic reaction after eating a cheese sandwich from the canteen. The sandwich was made with seeded bread (containing sesame seeds), which had been substituted for white bread in the most recent stock order.

(b) List **four** possible symptoms of an allergic reaction.

1. ....

2. ....

3. ....

4. ....

[4]

Cactus Summer Camp is reviewing its working practices after the incident with Finlay.

(c) Discuss the actions that the canteen staff should take to prevent cross-contamination of allergens in the future.

....

....

....

....

....

....

....

....

....

....

....

....

[6]

Exam Tip

For exam questions like part (c), there are lots of things you can talk about. It can help if you think through the entire process, from the storage of the ingredients to the serving of a meal, and what could go wrong at each step.

Mixed Questions 7 — Westoe

7 Westoe is a coastal town in the south of England. Tourism in the area has greatly increased after it won the 'Best Beach of the Year' award. The council has carried out a survey to understand which demographic groups visit the town.

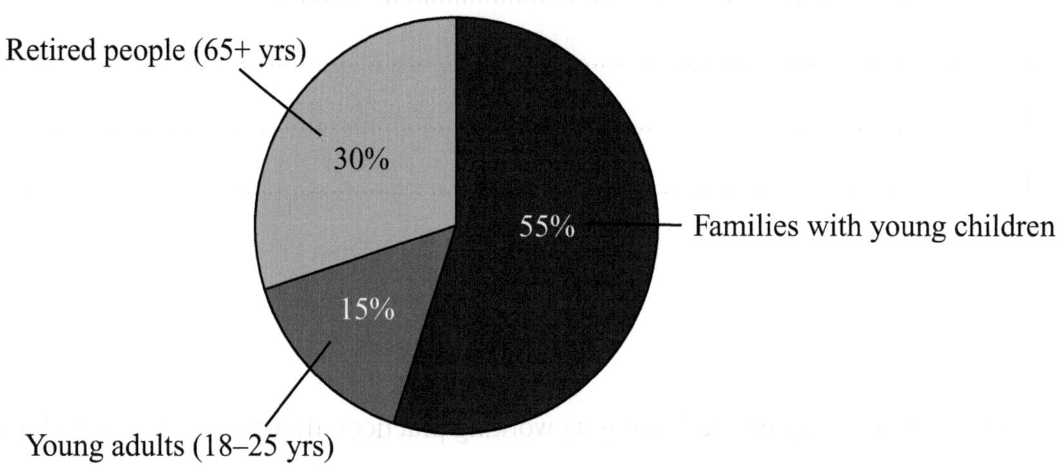

(a) State **one** type of accommodation that would meet the needs of each group identified in the survey. Choose a different type of accommodation for each group, justifying each of your answers.

Retired people: ....

....

....

....

Families with young children: ....

....

....

....

....

Young adults: ....

....

....

....

....

[6]

Mixed Questions 7 — Westoe

Many hospitality and catering establishments in Westoe close over winter.
This means employees are often on seasonal contracts.

(b) Give **two** disadvantages for an employee on a seasonal contract.

1. ....

....

2. ....

....

[2]

The Gallagher family plan to visit Westoe during the school summer holidays.
They plan to stay for one week. They have three children, aged ten, six and one.

(c) Discuss the **catering** establishments that would help to meet the needs of the Gallagher family.

....

....

....

....

....

....

....

....

....

....

....

....

....

....

....

....

[6]

Exam Tip

For 'Justify' questions (like part (a) on page 60), you'll need to explain why your answer is correct or reasonable. You might have to back up your answer using evidence from the context, or rely on knowledge from the course.

Mixed Questions 8 — Hoad House

8 Craig is the owner of Hoad House, a three-star guest house.

> The establishment has:
> - well-presented rooms, but only some are en-suite.
> - a small restaurant that offers a limited range of breakfast and dinner options.
> - free Wi-Fi® in all rooms and public areas.

(a) Review the information above, and suggest steps Craig should take to achieve a five-star rating.

....

....

....

....

....

....

....

....

[4]

(b) Discuss the impacts that a five-star rating would be likely to have on Hoad House.

....

....

....

....

....

....

....

....

....

....

....

....

[6]

Mixed Questions 8 — Hoad House

Craig is passionate about the environment and would like the guest house to be as environmentally friendly as possible. He is keen on making the guest house more sustainable by saving energy and water and reducing waste.

(c) Suggest **three** changes that could be made to reduce the guest house's environmental impact:

(i) by the housekeeping team

1. ....

....

2. ....

....

3. ....

....

[3]

(ii) by the front of house team

1. ....

....

2. ....

....

3. ....

....

[3]

(iii) by the kitchen brigade

1. ....

....

2. ....

....

3. ....

....

[3]

Exam Tip

'Front of house' refers to the part of a hotel or restaurant that the customer will see and where staff **directly** interact with customers. Think of it like the stage in a theatre. This of course means that 'back of house' is the behind-the-scenes area — back of house staff include chefs, finance, administrators, cleaners and maintenance workers.

Mixed Questions 9 — Biddick Hotel and Spa

9 Biddick Hotel and Spa has a website through which customers can make a booking.

(a) Other than the internet, list **two** forms of media.

1. ....

2. ....

[2]

Biddick Hotel and Spa is considering using social media to promote the business.

(b) Evaluate the use of social media to promote Biddick Hotel and Spa. You should discuss both the advantages and the disadvantages in your answer before forming a conclusion.

....

[8]

Biddick Hotel and Spa also uses media to recruit new staff.
They are about to advertise for a new front of house manager.

(c) Give **two** personal attributes the Biddick Hotel and Spa would look for in the new manager.

1. ....

2. ....

[2]

Mixed Questions 9 — Biddick Hotel and Spa

Biddick Hotel and Spa has received this online review from a recent guest.

A terrible experience ★☆☆☆☆ *review by Mrs Scott*

I am a wheelchair user, but there were no accessibility adjustments for those with disabilities in any area of the hotel (car park, reception, rooms and pool). I am deeply disappointed and will not stay here again.

(d) (i) Explain **one** negative impact that this review may have on the Biddick Hotel and Spa.

....

....

....

....

[2]

(ii) Discuss the changes that the Biddick Hotel and Spa should make to prevent similar reviews in the future.

....

....

....

....

....

....

....

....

....

....

....

....

....

[6]

Exam Tip

Meeting the needs of customers is essential to an establishment's success... but it's also the law — a business must make reasonable adjustments to accommodate the needs of guests with disabilities, under the Equality Act (2010).

Mixed Questions 10 — Rose and Crown Inn

10 Parvati is the owner of the Rose and Crown Inn, a small pub with some guest rooms. All room bookings are made over the phone and recorded on paper. Guests check-in at the main bar which means they often have to wait for service at busy times.

(a) Recommend **two** ways that technology could improve the customer experience when booking or checking in at the pub.

Recommendation 1: ....

....

....

....

Recommendation 2: ....

....

....

....

[4]

David, the head chef, is frustrated by the system used to communicate food orders to him. The waiting staff write down food orders on paper and deliver the orders to him directly. Mistakes often happen and the order is sometimes delayed in reaching him.

(b) Explain how technology may be used to support David.

....

....

....

....

....

....

....

....

[4]

Exam Tip

EPOS = Electronic Point of Sale. Think of an EPOS system as a digital cash register. You might have seen touch screen kiosks in places like fast food restaurants, but EPOS systems can do much more than take customer orders — they also record sales, monitor stock levels and allow customers to submit feedback. All good stuff for a business.

Answers

Questions with banded marking

Some questions are marked using bands, which describe an answer that is worth a certain number of marks. You need to judge which band description best matches your answer — this will give you an indication of the number of marks your answer would get.

If a band covers a range of marks (e.g. 3-4 marks), consider whether your answer is closer to the band above or to the band below to decide how many marks it's worth.

4 mark question
How to grade your answer:

4 marks: A very good response which shows a highly developed understanding of the topic in the question.
3 marks: A good response which shows a developed understanding of the topic in the question.
2 marks: A basic response which shows some understanding of the topic in the question.
1 mark: A limited response which may be a list of bullet points.
0 marks: There is no relevant information.

6 mark question
How to grade your answer:

5-6 marks: A very good response which shows a developed understanding that is relevant to the question.
3-4 marks: A good response which shows some understanding that is relevant to the question.
1-2 marks: A basic response which may be a list of bullet points.
0 marks: There is no relevant information.

8 mark question
How to grade your answer:

7-8 marks: An excellent response which demonstrates a developed understanding that is relevant to the question. For an evaluate question, this would include detailed judgments that are well-supported.
5-6 marks: A very good response which shows a developed understanding that is mainly relevant to the question. For an evaluate question, this would include judgments that are not fully supported.
3-4 marks: A good response which shows some understanding that is relevant to the question. For an evaluate question, this would include simple, unsupported judgments.
1-2 marks: A basic response which shows a simple understanding of the topic. It may be a list of bullet points.
0 marks: There is no relevant information.

Section 1.1 — Hospitality and Catering Provision

Pages 4-5: Commercial and Non-Commercial Provision

1

Residential	Non-residential
hostel care home	mobile food van factory canteen

[4 marks available — 1 mark for each correct answer placed]

2 Any three from: e.g. hospital / hospice / care home / boarding school / college / army barracks / prison / work canteen / food bank / soup kitchen
[3 marks available — 1 mark for each example]

3 (a) guest house / B&B / hostel ***[1 mark]***
(b) E.g. fast food restaurant / sandwich shop/deli ***[1 mark]***

4 Any three from: e.g. gym / fitness centre / spa / swimming pool
[3 marks available — 1 mark for each example]

5

	True	False
An aim of a coffee shop is usually to make a profit.	✓	
A cruise ship is an example of commercial non-residential provision.		✓
Non-commercial establishments do not aim to make a profit.	✓	

[3 marks available — 1 mark for each correct row]

6 (a) E.g. They could place food stalls or trucks around the park. / They could put vending machines in popular areas. / They could have cafés and restaurants in a food court.
[2 marks available — 1 mark for each way]
(b) Any one from: e.g. stadium / concert hall / museum ***[1 mark]***

7 E.g. The hotel would likely have a large conference room to cater for lots of people. / The hotel may supply equipment for presentations such as a projector. / The hotel can provide food and refreshments for the people attending.
[2 marks available — 1 mark for each reason]

Pages 6-7: Types of Food Service

1 Any three from: plate service / guéridon service / silver service / banquet / family-style
[3 marks available — 1 mark for each type]

2 E.g. Customers get a lot of dishes, so there should be something for everyone. / Customers serve themselves, so they can control the portion size. ***[1 mark]***

3 (a) (i) Customers can place an order at the counter, which will be quicker than waiting for staff to take their order at the table. ***[1 mark]***
(ii) Establishments can serve lots of customers in a short period of time. ***[1 mark]***
(b) Any one from: e.g. tray service / trolley service / vending service / takeaway ***[1 mark]***

4 Any two from: e.g. the restaurant may not have the necessary specialist equipment / staff may not have the required training or skills / it is slower than traditional plate service
[2 marks available — 1 mark for each reason]

5 You may have included some of these points in your answer:
Plate service and silver service are both types of table service.
For plate service, food is plated in the kitchen.
Waiting staff take plated food to the customer's table.
For silver service, food is not plated in the kitchen.
Waiting staff serve food from a large dish using a (silver) spoon and fork onto the customer's plate at the table.
Plate service is a very common type of food service in restaurants.
Silver service is a luxury food service that is only used in high-end establishments.
[Banded mark question — 4 marks available. See the start of this page for advice on how to mark your answer.]

6 E.g. A customer should expect to pick up any food and cold drinks they want from a long counter. They may have to order hot drinks at the till. They pay at the till and take cutlery back to their table.
[2 marks for a well developed outline like this, 1 mark if your answer is more basic]

7 E.g. Plate service
Guests can all be served at a similar time while food is still hot.
There will be consistent portion sizes across the dishes.
[3 marks available — 1 mark for a suitable type of food service, 1 mark for each reason]
Buffets are also popular at weddings which are usually a more casual, cheaper option than table service.

Page 8: Standards and Ratings

1

	True	False
Michelin stars are awarded based on the standard of service only.		✓
The highest number of Michelin stars is three.	✓	
Michelin stars can be awarded to individual chefs.		✓

[3 marks available — 1 mark for each correct row]

Michelin stars are based on the quality of the dishes, not the service. They are only awarded to restaurants, not individual chefs.

2 E.g. There could be fewer repeat customers to the restaurant because they could be concerned that the quality of the food and service has decreased.
[2 marks for a well developed outline like this, 1 mark if your answer is more basic]

3 You may have included some of these points in your answer:
The Red Drake may not offer breakfast or dinner every day. If they do, the food options will likely be limited.
The Blue Dragon would serve breakfast and dinner every day, and offer a range of higher-quality food options.
The Red Drake would have basic accommodation and minimum levels of cleanliness.
The Blue Dragon would have luxury accommodation and exceptional levels of cleanliness.
The service at the Red Drake would be informal.
The service at the Blue Dragon would be professional and personalised.
The Blue Dragon would offer extra services, such as valet parking and 24/7 room service.
[Banded mark question — 4 marks available. See page 67 for advice on how to mark your answer.]

Pages 9-11: Employment Roles and Qualifications

1 Any two from: chambermaid / cleaner / maintenance staff / caretaker ***[2 marks available — 1 mark for each role]***

2 Any three from: e.g. Level 1/2 Vocational Award in Hospitality and Catering / BTEC in Hospitality or Catering / Bachelor's Degree in Catering / HND in Professional Cookery / GCSE Food Preparation and Nutrition / first aid certificate / health and safety certificate / food hygiene certificate
[3 marks available — 1 mark for each qualification]

3

Front of house	Back of house
waiting staff valet	kitchen porter pastry chef

[4 marks available — 1 mark for each correct answer placed]

4 E.g. A front of house manager hires and trains front of house staff. They will delegate jobs to their team and ensure that they are done to a high standard.
[2 marks for a well developed outline like this, 1 mark if your answer is more basic]

5 (a) Marketing manager ***[1 mark]***
(b) E.g. They could target certain groups with special offers or discounts. ***[1 mark]***

6 Any two from: e.g. it provides income while you train / it helps you gain useful skills and experience / it helps you gain a recognised qualification / it helps you know whether you would like working in the catering industry
[2 marks available — 1 mark for each benefit]

7

Role	Key responsibility
Executive / head chef	E.g. plans the menu / hires and trains chefs / orders ingredients and equipment
↓ Sous-chef	Oversees kitchen staff.
↓ Chef de partie	In charge of one area of the kitchen, e.g. sauce, soup, vegetables, fish.
↓ Commis chef	Helps other chefs with easier tasks.

[4 marks available — 1 mark for each correct role, 1 mark for each key responsibility]

8 (a) Any three from: e.g. greeting customers / training waiting staff / supervising waiting staff / dealing with complaints / managing guest reservations
[3 marks available — 1 mark for each responsibility]
(b) Any two from: e.g. good leadership skills / good communication skills / good organisational skills / politeness / able to work under pressure
[2 marks available — 1 mark for each skill or attribute]

9 Any one from: e.g. A concierge helps guests to book tourist attractions, reservations and taxis in the local area. / A valet welcomes guests to the hotel and parks their car.
[2 marks for a well developed outline like one of these, 1 mark if your answer is more basic]
1-star hotels are unlikely to employ concierges or valets, but 5-star hotels need roles like these to go the extra mile and deliver the best service that they can for their guests.

10 You may have included some of these points in your answer:
They oversee the front of house and kitchen to make sure jobs are completed to a sufficient standard.
They are responsible for the day-to-day provision of food and drink at the establishment.
They manage bookings to ensure that the establishment will make sufficient money without overworking staff.
They pay any bills, such as water and rent.
They order stock, such as napkins and glasses.
They ensure customers are happy with their experience.
They train staff and maintain health and safety standards.
[Banded mark question — 4 marks available. See page 67 for advice on how to mark your answer.]

Page 12: Contracts and Working Hours

1 Any two from: e.g. they have holiday entitlement / they receive sick pay / they receive a salary / they receive a pension / they work a fixed number of hours
[2 marks available — 1 mark for each advantage]

2 (a) E.g. A temporary contract is a contract with a fixed end date/fixed period. ***[1 mark]***
(b) E.g. She does not have long-term job security. / She may have limited career progression/development opportunities. ***[1 mark]***

3 E.g. Employees cannot work more than an average of 48 hours a week, unless they choose to.
If shifts are over 6 hours, employees are entitled to a 20-minute break and at least one day off a week.
[2 marks available — 1 mark for each law]

4 E.g. Seasonal
Students would be busy studying during term-times, so a seasonal contract over the summer holidays would be suitable for them as they would have fewer commitments during this time.
[2 marks available — 1 mark for a suitable contract, 1 mark for a justification]

Page 13: Pay and Benefits

1 (a) The legal minimum amount that employers must pay employees per hour. ***[1 mark]***
(b) E.g. A salary is a fixed amount paid to an employee every month. The amount paid doesn't change if an employee works more or fewer hours than in their contract.
[2 marks for a well developed outline like this, 1 mark if your answer is more basic]
(c) Any one from: e.g. they want more pay / they want to receive more benefits ***[1 mark]***

2 Any two from: e.g. He may earn tips from his customers as extra money. / He may be offered extra pay (e.g. double pay) to work over busy periods, such as Christmas. / He may receive a bonus or vouchers as an appreciation for his hard work or if the restaurant is performing well. / He may get a free staff meal or a staff discount on meals.
[2 marks available — 1 mark for each benefit]

Pages 14-15: Costs, Profits and Economic Impact

1 Labour costs, which is the total amount paid in wages, payroll taxes and any other employee benefits.
Material costs, which will include ingredients and drinks, and other consumables that customers and staff use like napkins and cleaning materials.
Overhead costs, which will be the regular bills that need to be paid to keep the establishment running,

such as rent, electricity, water and gas.
[6 marks available — 1 mark for each cost, 1 mark for each linked explanation]

2 (a) She makes a positive gross profit, because the selling price is more than the cost of the ingredients to make the dish (£12 – £3 = £9 profit).
[2 marks available — 1 mark for positive gross profit, 1 mark for a linked justification]

(b) This dish is considered non-essential, so customers must pay an extra 20% VAT on it which goes to the government to pay for public services etc.
[2 marks for a well developed outline like this, 1 mark if your answer is more basic]

3 E.g. People have more disposable income, so they are more likely to spend more on eating out. This means hospitality businesses receive more money and profits.
[2 marks for a well developed outline like this, 1 mark if your answer is more basic]
You could also mention that overheads and material costs will likely be cheaper for businesses.

4 (a) He would have a negative net profit, because his total costs were more than his food sales (£5000 – £6000 = –£1000 profit).
[2 marks available — 1 mark for negative net profit, 1 mark for a linked justification]

(b) Any four from: e.g. he could see whether importing ingredients is cheaper / he could buy lower quality, cheaper relishes / he could charge customers for adding a relish / he could do more advertising to aim to increase food sales / he could increase the selling price of his burgers
[4 marks available — 1 mark for each action]

Page 16: Environmental Impacts

1 (a) Any two from: e.g. use the correct sized pans / put lids on pans when boiling water / don't boil more water than is needed / fully load dishwashers
[2 marks available — 1 mark for each way]

(b) Any two from: e.g. reduce the number of times bedding is changed / encourage guests to use towels more than once / only heat occupied rooms / install motion-sensing lights
[2 marks available — 1 mark for each way]

2 Any two from: e.g. seasonal foods will often be fresher / seasonal foods will have a smaller carbon footprint / environmentally-conscious customers may be persuaded to book at the restaurant
[2 marks available — 1 mark for each benefit]

3 Any three from: e.g. order ingredients in bulk to reduce packaging / avoid suppliers who use non-recyclable packaging / rotate stock to avoid it going out of date (FIFO) / prepare the correct amount of food / encourage customers to take home leftovers / donate leftover ingredients to charity / compost leftover food that cannot be donated / reuse containers for storage / reuse leftover ingredients in other dishes, e.g. stocks
[3 marks available — 1 mark for each action]

Page 17: The Impact of Technology

1 (a) Any one from: e.g. He won't have to keep cash in the café, which could reduce the risk of theft. / He won't have to visit the bank to deposit cash, which will save him time.
[2 marks for a well developed outline like one of these, 1 mark if your answer is more basic]

(b) Any two from: e.g. using a contactless card / using a digital wallet or app on a smartphone / paying online through a website / scanning a QR code
[2 marks available — 1 mark for each way]

2 You may have included some of these points in your answer:
Hotels may offer online or self-service check-in options which would speed up service for customers.
Hotels may have key cards for rooms, which can be stored in a wallet so are easier to carry around than traditional keys.
Hotels may issue wristbands or room keys that can be used for payment. This means guests do not need to carry cash or bank cards around with them.
Hotels may display information about entertainment schedules or menus on an app or website. This allows guests to access up-to-date information from any location.
Hotels may have an app that allows guests to book dinner reservations or other activities at a time convenient to them.
[Banded mark question — 4 marks available. See page 67 for advice on how to mark your answer.]

3 Any one from: e.g. Staff can input a food order into an EPOS system, which records the order and can create a final bill. / Stock control systems monitor stock levels and can re-order stock automatically when stock is running low. / Booking systems record table or room bookings, and can prevent a staff member from double-booking.
[2 marks for a well developed outline like one of these, 1 mark if your answer is more basic]

Page 18: The Impact of Media

1 E.g. An establishment could run a competition on their website or social media page. Many people would engage with the competition, generating a lot of interest in the business.
[2 marks for a well developed outline like this, 1 mark if your answer is more basic]

2 Advantage: e.g. social media can be used for free, so he won't have to budget for any advertising costs.
Disadvantage: e.g. he may not reach certain demographic groups, such as elderly people.
[2 marks available — 1 mark for an advantage, 1 mark for a disadvantage]

3 (a) Office Elves could pay for an advert in a business magazine to reach their target audience or deliver leaflets to specific local businesses.
[2 marks for a well developed outline like this, 1 mark if your answer is more basic]

(b) Office Elves could make a radio advert to promote their business and have it air during peak times for business commuters, such as morning rush hour.
[2 marks for a well developed outline like this, 1 mark if your answer is more basic]

Section 1.2 — How Providers Operate

Pages 19-20: Operational Requirements

1 Any three from: e.g. reception / bar / restaurant / waiting area
[3 marks available — 1 mark for each area]

2 First missing stage: Delivery is checked/recorded
Second missing stage: Food is prepared/cooked
[2 marks available — 1 mark for each stage]

3 (a) Any two from: e.g. take payment / record customer details / issue room keys/key cards / direct customers to their rooms.
[2 marks available — 1 mark for each responsibility]

(b) You may have included some of these points in your answer:
Reception need to inform housekeeping when guests are arriving in each room. This allows decisions to be made about which rooms to clean first.
Housekeeping need to inform reception when rooms are ready. This information prevents keys being issued to uncleaned rooms.
If a guest contacts reception about something they need, such as extra towels, reception must be able to communicate the request to housekeeping swiftly so that customers receive good service.
Housekeeping need to inform reception of items guests need to be charged for, such as minibar contents. Failing to do this will damage the profits of the business.
[Banded mark question — 4 marks available. See page 67 for advice on how to mark your answer.]

4 You may have included some of these points in your answer:
Both types of restaurant will have seating areas for diners.
Both types of restaurant need a storage area where staff can access things such as extra napkins or sauces.
In table service restaurants, there is often a waiting area for customers to sit in if their table isn't ready. In counter service

restaurants, people usually seat themselves at a free table.
In table service restaurants, the dining area may be divided up into zones so that each member of staff knows which tables they are responsible for.
In counter service restaurants, there are counters of food from which customers can help themselves. In table service restaurants, there is an area where waiting staff collect plated up food.
In counter service restaurants, there will be a payment area.
In table service restaurants, a member of staff takes payment at the table.
[Banded mark question — 4 marks available. See page 67 for advice on how to mark your answer.]

5 (a) Each station is close to the next one in the order of workflow. This means staff do not have to move around too much so are less likely to bump into each other when carrying hot liquids.
[2 marks for a well developed outline like this, 1 mark if your answer is more basic]
(b) Separate preparation areas for ingredients that contain allergens, e.g. nuts, to reduce the risk of allergen-free dishes being contaminated.
[2 marks for a well developed outline like this, 1 mark if your answer is more basic]

6 Any two from: e.g. so that staff have a safe location to store their bags and coats / so that staff can get changed into their uniforms / so that staff can take a break away from customers
[2 marks available — 1 mark for each reason]

Pages 21-22: Equipment, Materials and Dress Code

1 E.g.
Task: Food storage
Piece of equipment: Walk-in fridge-freezer
How it improves efficiency: Staff can find the ingredients they need quickly.
Task: Food preparation
Piece of equipment: Floor-standing mixer
How it improves efficiency: It allows large quantities of, e.g. dough, to be made quickly.
Task: Cleaning dishes and utensils
Piece of equipment: Pass-through dishwasher
How it improves efficiency: It doesn't need to be emptied before next load is put in.
[6 marks available — 1 mark for each piece of equipment, 1 mark for each linked benefit]

2

Preparation	Cooking
chopping board measuring jug	spatula baking tray

[4 marks available — 1 mark for each piece of equipment correctly placed]

3 Any three from: e.g. first aid kit / fire extinguisher / fire blanket / carbon monoxide detectors / smoke alarm.
[3 marks available — 1 mark for each piece of equipment]

4 Any one from: e.g. High quality equipment should last longer than lower quality equipment. This means that money will be saved in the long term as the business will not have to replace items so often. / High quality equipment is likely to work more efficiently. This means that tasks will be carried out in a shorter time, saving money on labour costs.
[2 marks for a well developed outline like one of these, 1 mark if your answer is more basic]

5 Item: Hat
Purpose: Prevents hairs/sweat getting into food.
Item: Jacket/chef whites
Purpose: Protects against scalds.
Item: Oven gloves
Purpose: Handling hot trays/dishes.
[6 marks available — 1 mark for each item, 1 mark for each purpose]

6 You may have included some of these points in your answer:
Front of house staff are often required to wear a uniform so that they look smart and professional.
Rules about clean clothing/good hygiene are set so that staff make a good impression on customers.
A uniform means that staff can easily be identified. This shows customers who they should approach for assistance.
Rules about jewellery/hair may be set so that staff project the correct brand image.
[Banded mark question — 4 marks available. See page 67 for advice on how to mark your answer.]

Page 23: Administration and Documentation

1

	True	False
Only large businesses need to report major injuries to HSE.		✓
Businesses with more than 10 employees must keep records of all injuries.	✓	

[2 marks available — 1 mark for each correctly placed tick]

2 Any one from: e.g. Stock control can be complicated and take a long time for a person to do. A computer system is much quicker so fewer labour hours are needed. / Computerised stock control systems can monitor how stock levels of many items change over time. This means they can calculate how much stock should be ordered more easily than a person. / Stock control systems can automatically reorder stock when necessary. This means that items should never run out.
[2 marks for a well developed outline like one of these, 1 mark if your answer is more basic]

3 E.g. The yoghurt with the 18 Mar use by date must be stored behind the other yoghurt. This means older stock will be used first.
[2 marks for a well developed outline like this, 1 mark if your answer is more basic]
You might've outlined what First In, First Out (FIFO) means. That's OK as long as you talk about how they're stored, e.g. the yoghurt that's 'first in' will be stored at the front so it gets used first.

4 You may have included some of these points in your answer:
The delivery should be checked to make sure the correct items and quantities have been received. If they haven't, the supplier will need to correct the problem somehow, e.g. by delivering the missing items or by issuing a refund.
Identifying items that are missing from a delivery allows a menu change to be planned if the usual dishes can't be offered.
The delivery should be checked for spoiled goods, or those beyond their use by date. These goods should be rejected so they don't need to be paid for.
The delivery should be checked for damaged packaging. This could have allowed the contents to become contaminated.
Some items must be kept within a certain temperature range. If the temperature is too high, bacteria in the food could have multiplied to dangerous levels.
[Banded mark question — 4 marks available. See page 67 for advice on how to mark your answer.]

Pages 24-25: Meeting Customer Needs

1 (a) E.g. Establishments can allow local residents to pay to use leisure facilities, such as the swimming pool or spa.
[2 marks for a well developed outline like this, 1 mark if your answer is more basic]
(b) You may have included some of these points in your answer:
Both groups of customers would require a clean, comfortable and safe environment.
Both groups want good value for money.
Both groups require accessibility.
Business customers may need rooms to be equipped with items such as a trouser press and a desk.
Leisure customers with children might require a family room, or equipment such as a cot.
Business customers may require a quicker breakfast at an earlier time.
Leisure customers may prefer to have breakfast at a later time.
Business customers may require conference facilities.
Leisure customers may prefer access to a swimming pool or spa.
[Banded mark question — 4 marks available. See page 67 for advice on how to mark your answer.]

2 Consumer Rights Act — The Chicken Kiev was not as described on the menu.
Equality Act — The customer was given fewer chips due to their gender. This is discrimination.
[4 marks available — 1 mark for identifying each correct set of laws, 1 mark for each linked reason]

3 You may have included some of these points in your answer:
Businesses could provide Braille signage. This would allow visually impaired customers to navigate the premises more easily.
Hearing loops could be added, e.g. in reception areas or conference rooms, so that people with hearing difficulties can hear what is being said.
Ramps/lifts could be installed. This would allow guests in wheelchairs to gain access to all parts of the building.
Fully accessible rooms could be made available for guests with disabilities, e.g. with wider doorways, lower sinks and grab handles.
Hoists/special changing rooms could be provided at the pool so that disabled people can use it.
[Banded mark question — 4 marks available. See page 67 for advice on how to mark your answer.]
There are loads of adaptations you could put in response to this question. The trick is to develop each point with a bit of explanation.

4 E.g.
Allergens should be clearly labelled on the menu. This would mean customers would know whether they were safe to order a certain dish.
Waiting staff could ask guests if they have any allergies before they take an order so that they can alert guests if the dish they order is unsuitable.
[4 marks available — 1 mark for each basic recommendation, 2 marks for each more developed recommendation]

5 You may have included some of these points in your answer:
If customer needs are met, the customer is likely to return to the business and spend more money. This will be good for the profits of the business.
If customer needs are met, they will leave positive reviews online. This is a free form of advertising which may bring in additional customers.
Meeting customer needs can help a business stand out from their competitors, meaning customers choose to go to them rather than other establishments.
Meeting the needs of disabled customers is a legal requirement for businesses. Failing to do so may mean they face legal action.
[Banded mark question — 4 marks available. See page 67 for advice on how to mark your answer.]

Page 26: Customer Expectations

1 You may have included some of these points in your answer:
Both groups of customers would expect a clean, safe environment.
Both groups of customers would expect good value for money.
Both groups of customers would expect the accommodation and facilities to be accessible to them.
Guests at a luxury hotel are likely to expect higher quality linens and towels than a guest at a budget guest house.
A guest at a luxury hotel is likely to expect additional services, such as room service/a porter to take their luggage to their room. A guest at a budget guest house would expect to have to leave their room to get food/carry their own luggage.
A guest at a luxury hotel is likely to expect modern technology such as free high-speed Wi-Fi. A guest at a budget guest house would expect to have to pay extra for Wi-Fi.
[Banded mark question — 4 marks available. See page 67 for advice on how to mark your answer.]

2 Any three from: e.g. dishes made from local ingredients / use of seasonal ingredients / a good range of plant-based dishes / online menus/receipts / no single-use plastic / energy-efficient lighting
[3 marks available — 1 mark for each expectation]

3 Any one from: e.g. Social media can raise guests' expectations of a hotel, e.g. if there are lots of 5 star reviews. / Social media can make guests expect an excellent service, e.g. if an influencer has stayed there and reported on the great service that they received. / Guests may have expectations about how their room will look because of photos of rooms that have been shared on social media.
[2 marks for a well developed outline like one of these, 1 mark if your answer is more basic]

4 E.g. They should keep up with changing trends so that they can make changes to their services to stay competitive.
[2 marks for a well developed outline like this, 1 mark if your answer is more basic]

Page 27: Customer Demographics

1 (a) E.g. Families with children ***[1 mark]***
(b) Any two from: e.g. a play area near the dining area so that children will be entertained while their parents eat / a swimming pool so that families have something to do in the evening / a children's menu with dishes that will appeal to children at a low price / childminding services so that parents can go out in the evening.
[4 marks available. For each facility or service give 2 marks for a well developed outline like one of these, 1 mark if your answer is more basic]

2 (a) Restaurants ***[1 mark]***
(b) E.g. Target market: People with high incomes
Reason: This market is likely to be willing to spend more money on eating out in the hope of better food/service.
[2 marks available — 1 mark for a target market, 1 mark for a reason]

Section 1.3 — Health & Safety

Pages 28-29: Health and Safety Laws

1 (a) Any two from: e.g. Assess which risks can be avoided with PPE / remind employees to wear PPE / store PPE correctly
[2 marks available — 1 mark for each]
(b) E.g. Wear any provided PPE / attend training about the use of PPE ***[1 mark]***

2 (a) E.g. To reduce the risk of physical injuries from lifting and carrying heavy objects in the workplace.
[2 marks for a well developed outline like this, 1 mark if your answer is more basic]
(b)

Stage	What employee must do
Assess the situation	Check how heavy the object is / check for hazards / ask for help to move object
Lift the object	Bend knees / squat with feet either side of object / keep back straight / keep object close to body
Carry the object	Keep object close to body / make sure they can say where they are going

[3 marks available — 1 mark for each row]

3 E.g. Employers must record and report health and safety incidents that caused or had potential to cause death, serious injury or disease to the Health and Safety Executive (HSE).
[2 marks for a well developed outline like this, 1 mark if your answer is more basic]

4 Any three from: e.g. put instructions learnt in training into practice / use correct safety equipment provided / report hazards to a manager / report any accidents or injuries
[3 marks available — 1 mark for each responsibility]
It'd be easy here to have listed employer responsibilities by mistake — read the question carefully. That one letter makes all the difference.

5 (a) E.g. A COSHH form should be completed. This lists the ways that the substance could be harmful and control measures that should be taken to reduce the risks.
[2 marks for a well developed outline like this, 1 mark if your answer is more basic]
You could have talked about a risk assessment form here. This also gives the control measures that should be taken to reduce the risk of harm from the substance.
(b) You may have included some of these points in your answer:
Provide correct storage, e.g. a locked cupboard.
Provide training for employees to make sure they know that the hazard symbol means the chemical is toxic.

Train employees about the actions they should take to stay safe when dealing with this chemical.
Provide suitable PPE, e.g. gloves and an apron.
Train employees on how to use PPE correctly.
[Banded mark question — 4 marks available. See page 67 for advice on how to mark your answer.]

Page 30: Accident Forms and Risk Assessments

1 (a) Any two from: e.g. wipe up spills immediately / display warning signs about wet floors / install non-slip flooring / provide kitchen staff with slip-resistant footwear.
[2 marks available — 1 mark for each]
(b) Any one from: e.g. to determine who was at fault in the accident / to identify patterns so that problems can be addressed / to identify risks so that similar injuries can be prevented from happening. *[1 mark]*

2 (a) E.g.

Hazard	Control measure
Bacteria may be present if food is undercooked.	Check food is cooked to over 75 °C using a probe.
Slipping on wet floor	Display warning signs
Food could be physically contaminated with plasters.	Kitchen staff must wear blue plasters.

[6 marks available — 1 mark for each hazard, 1 mark for a linked control measure]
(b) The level of risk is the likelihood of the hazard happening and causing harm. *[1 mark]*

Page 31: Hazard Analysis and Critical Control Points

1 (a) E.g. pips / bones / plastic / glass / fingernails *[1 mark]*
(b) chemical *[1 mark]*, biological *[1 mark]*

2 (a) Type of hazard: physical *[1 mark]*
How risk is reduced: Hairs are prevented from falling into food. *[1 mark]*
(b) Type of hazard: biological *[1 mark]*
How risk is reduced: Bacteria in the food are killed. *[1 mark]*
(c) Type of hazard: chemical *[1 mark]*
How risk is reduced: Cleaning products are prevented from getting into food. *[1 mark]*

3 E.g.

Hazard	Control point
Bacteria could grow on high-risk food.	Store high-risk food in a fridge or freezer when not being used and record fridge/freezer temperature regularly.

[2 marks available — 1 mark for one food storage hazard and 1 mark for a linked control point]

Section 1.4: Food Safety

Pages 32-34: Food-Induced Ill-Health

1 (a) E.g. A food intolerance is where someone cannot properly digest a type of food, which can lead to irritation of the digestive system and other symptoms.
[2 marks for a well developed outline like this, 1 mark if your answer is more basic]
(b) Any two from: e.g. bacteria / allergies / chemical contamination / physical contamination
[2 marks available — 1 mark for each cause]

2

Common allergen	Not a common allergen
molluscs, soya, mustard	ginger

[4 marks available — 1 mark for each correct answer placed]

3 (a) E.g. milk *[1 mark]*
(b) E.g. pasta *[1 mark]*
(c) E.g. diet soft drinks *[1 marks]*

4 (a) Any two from: e.g. anaphylactic shock / bloating / breathing difficulties / chills / diarrhoea / facial swelling / pale skin / rash / vomiting / weight loss
[2 marks available — 1 mark for each symptom]
(b) Any two from: e.g. constipation / feeling sick / painful joints / stomach ache / weakness / flatulence
[2 marks available — 1 mark for each symptom]

5 (a) Any one from: e.g. raw meat / raw vegetables / raw fruit *[1 mark]*
(b) Any one from: e.g. raw poultry / raw meat / untreated milk *[1 mark]*
(c) Any one from: e.g. soft cheese / pâté / shellfish *[1 mark]*

6 Any two from: e.g. bloating / stomach ache / weakness / diarrhoea
[2 marks available — 1 mark for each symptom]

7 E.g. Anaphylaxis is a severe allergic reaction. It can cause life-threatening symptoms, such as breathing difficulties, so must be treated in hospital immediately.
[2 marks for a well developed outline like this, 1 mark if your answer is more basic]
Many people with severe allergies carry an adrenaline auto-injector.

8 E.g. She didn't refrigerate the rice within 90 minutes of cooking it, so the rice could now have dangerous levels of *Bacillus cereus*, which can still remain in the food even after reheating.
[2 marks for a well developed outline like this, 1 mark if your answer is more basic]

9 E.g. If raw chicken juices were allowed to drip onto a cooked dish, then the dish could be contaminated with *Clostridium perfringens* because the bacteria is often found in raw meat/poultry, such as chicken.
[2 marks for a well developed outline like this, 1 mark if your answer is more basic]
Other causes include inadequately reheating food or leaving food to stand at room temperature for too long.

10 (a) Any two from: e.g. cereals (English muffin) / lupin (English muffin) / milk (butter) / eggs / fish (smoked salmon) / sulphites (lemon juice)
[2 marks available — 1 mark for each allergen]
(b) E.g. Bacteria: *Listeria*
Listeria can be found in smoked fish (salmon), so this bacteria could be present if the salmon was not correctly stored in the fridge or is past its use-by-date.
[2 marks available — 1 mark for a suitable bacteria, 1 mark for a linked explanation]

Pages 35-36: Preventing Food-Induced Ill-Health

1 Any one from: e.g. The waiting staff or a menu description should inform Ali of any dishes that contain nuts, so that he can choose other dishes or ask for substitutions to be made. / The kitchen staff should follow correct hygiene procedures to prevent cross-contamination of dishes that don't contain nuts with nuts.
[2 marks for a well developed outline like one of these, 1 mark if your answer is more basic]

2 E.g. The head chef should reject the delivery, as the prawns could be dangerous to eat. This is because the correct temperature for chilling foods is between 0 °C and 5 °C.
[2 marks for a well developed outline like this, 1 mark if your answer is more basic]

3 Any four from: e.g. keep raw food and cooked foods in separate containers / store raw meat or fish at the bottom of the fridge / wash raw fruit and vegetables thoroughly / use coloured chopping boards and knives for different food groups / regularly wash and sanitise surfaces and utensils
[4 marks available — 1 mark for each way]

4 (a) Hot buffet food should be kept above 63 °C. *[1 mark]*
(b) Frozen leftovers should be kept below –18 °C. *[1 mark]*

5 Any two from: e.g. wash hands regularly / wear a clean uniform / cover any cuts with a clean plaster / stay off work if they are ill
[2 marks available — 1 mark for each measure]
Staff should always wash their hands after handling high-risk foods, going to the toilet, sneezing or handling waste.

6 You may have included some of these points in your answer:
Keep areas clean and remove waste immediately to prevent pests, e.g. flies and rats, being attracted to the premises.
Ensure staff follow personal hygiene rules and wear appropriate PPE, e.g. hairnets to cover hair.
Check food deliveries for any broken packaging.
Keep food covered when it's not in use.
Monitor equipment for damage, replacing when necessary.

Use blue plasters to cover cuts, which can easily be spotted if they fall off.
Ensure staff remove jewellery/false nails/nail varnish etc.
[Banded mark question — 4 marks available. See page 67 for advice on how to mark your answer.]

Page 37: Catering and the Law

1 (a) Any two from: e.g. food they provide must be safe to eat / food must be described or advertised in an accurate way / the quality of food must be what customers expect
[2 marks available — 1 mark for each responsibility]
(b) E.g. Food Safety and Hygiene Regulations (2013) ***[1 mark]***

2 (a) (i) E.g. This information helps customers with allergies to make informed choices whether to use a condiment. Customers can avoid foods that could cause an allergic reaction and becoming ill.
[2 marks available — 1 mark for a reason, 1 mark for a linked justification]
(ii) E.g. This information lets Rahul know whether the product should be kept at room temperature or needs storing in the fridge. Correct storage will help to avoid food wastage, which could damage his profits.
[2 marks available — 1 mark for a reason, 1 mark for a linked justification]
(b) Any four from: e.g. the product name / list of ingredients / name and address of manufacturer / nutritional information / cooking instructions / weight or volume of product / a use-by or best-before date / country of origin / a warning if genetically modified ingredients have been used
[4 marks available — 1 mark for each piece of information]

Page 38: Role of the EHO

1 (a) E.g. An EHO is responsible for ensuring catering businesses are obeying food safety laws. They will inspect a premises and collect evidence, and can take actions to improve their hygiene.
[2 marks for a well developed outline like this, 1 mark if your answer is more basic]
(b) Any two from: e.g. the business is newly open / a complaint has been made against the business / there has been an accident in the workplace / there has been an outbreak of pests / there has been a food poisoning incident
[2 marks available — 1 mark for each reason]
(c) Any three from: e.g. check food handlers are wearing appropriate PPE / check food handlers have up-to-date certificates / check the premises is in good, clean condition / check equipment is safe to use / check mandatory health and safety signs are displayed / check food is safe to eat / check correct temperature control is used when storing food / check a HACCP plan is in place for hazards and risks
[3 marks available — 1 mark for each check]

2 Any three from: e.g. close the business if the risk to the public is high / impose fines / take legal action if laws have been broken / advise the business how to improve before a re-inspection
[3 marks available — 1 mark for each action]

Exam Skills 2

Page 42: Extended-Answer Questions

E.g. I would give this answer 8 marks out of 8, because it provides a wide range of detailed responsibilities which are relevant to the question. There are also examples to support the points made. Use of specific terminology, such as 'commis chef', is also accurate.

Section 2 — Mixed Questions

Pages 44-46: Yewbrook Care Home

1 (a) (i) You should have given **one** hazard and **one** suitable control point. Here are two example hazards:

	Hazard	Control point
Storage	E.g. Bacterial growth due to food being in the danger zone.	E.g. Refrigerate/freeze chicken as soon as possible. / Only remove chicken from fridge at time of preparation. / Check fridge temperature is 0 to 5 °C. / Check freezer temperature is -18 °C or less.
	E.g. Food expired (past 'use-by' date).	E.g. Check use-by date. / Label chicken clearly with 'use-by' date. / Use FIFO (first in, first out) rotation/use oldest food first.

[2 marks available — 1 mark for a hazard and 1 mark for a suitable control point]
Other storage hazards include: raw chicken being stored on incorrect shelf could cross-contaminate other foods and damaged packaging could mean bacteria multiply faster on the chicken.

(ii) You should have given **one** hazard and **one** suitable control point. Here are two example hazards:

	Hazard	Control point
Preparation	E.g. Cross-contamination via equipment (e.g. chopping boards and knives).	E.g. Use separate utensils to prepare raw and cooked foods. / Use colour-coded chopping board (red for raw meat).
	E.g. Chemical contamination from cleaning products.	E.g. Don't use sprays/ cleaning equipment around food.

Other preparation hazards relating to raw chicken include: it being in the danger zone too long before cooking, cross-contamination of ready-to-eat/cooked/fresh foods and physical contamination from broken equipment.
[2 marks available — 1 mark for a hazard and 1 mark for a suitable control point]

(iii) You should have given **one** hazard and **one** suitable control point. Here are two example hazards:

	Hazard	Control point
Cooking	E.g. Bacteria could survive being cooked.	E.g. Core temperature of food should be over 75 °C for at least 3 minutes.
	E.g. Food could be contaminated if the same utensils are used for both raw food and cooked food.	E.g. Wash equipment with hot soapy water between tasks. / Keep utensils used for raw food separate to those used for cooked food.

Other cooking hazards include: physical contamination from broken equipment/packaging, physical contamination from staff (e.g. hair/nails) and allergenic contamination.
[2 marks available — 1 mark for a hazard and 1 mark for a suitable control point]

(iv) You should have given **one** hazard and **one** suitable control point. Here are two example hazards:

	Hazard	Control point
Serving	E.g. Hot food not kept at adequate temperature (63 °C +).	E.g. Maintain hot holding temperature (63 °C) using a Bain-Marie/heat lamp/food warming station.
	E.g. Food is contaminated with allergens when serving.	E.g. Use separate utensils for different foods. / Cover foods that are prepared as allergen-free (e.g. gluten free). / Label foods with allergens.

Other serving hazards include: food being left out for longer than two hours and using utensils to serve food that have been used previously with raw food.
[2 marks available — 1 mark for a hazard and 1 mark for a suitable control point]

(b) (i) Any two from: e.g. *Campylobacter / E. coli / Salmonella*
[2 marks available — 1 mark for each named bacteria]
You need to make sure you only give examples of bacteria that can be found in raw poultry.

(ii)

Bacteria	Visible symptom	Non-visible symptom
Campylobacter	E.g. diarrhoea / vomiting	E.g. feeling sick / fever
E. coli	E.g. diarrhoea / vomiting	E.g. stomach ache / fever
Salmonella	E.g. diarrhoea / vomiting	E.g. feeling sick / fever

[2 marks available — 1 mark for a visible symptom and 1 mark for a non-visible symptom]

(c) (i) ***[2 marks available — 1 mark for each description of a way that* Staphylococcus aureus *can contaminate food]***

(ii) ***[2 marks available — 1 mark for each control measure]***
Example answers are shown in the table below.

Contamination hazard	How to control the risk
E.g. The person preparing the food can have the bacteria on their skin. They may transfer the bacteria using their hands if they touch food.	E.g. Staff should wash their hands regularly, to reduce the chance of harmful bacteria being present on their skin.
E.g. The person preparing the food might have the bacteria in their nose or mouth. They might cough or sneeze over the food and contaminate it.	E.g. Staff should be told not to come into work if they are feeling ill to reduce the chance of them coughing or sneezing onto food.

There are lots of points you could give for this question but they must be all be relevant to Staphylococcus aureus.

(d) You may have included some of these points in your answer:
<u>During the inspection</u>
The EHO will check the record books/HACCP records that keep track of things like fridge temperatures, cleaning schedules, staff training and pest control visits.
By checking the records books the EHO can identify if any of the staff aren't sufficiently trained / if fridges haven't been maintained at temperatures safe for food storage.
The EHO will observe the food service staff to see if they are following food safety legislation, for example washing their hands frequently enough.
The EHO will check working practices to check food is being prepared and served in a safe way and correctly stored.
For example, the EHO may probe food to check it is being heated to the correct temperature (at least 75 °C) and for long enough.
The EHO will also check the establishment to make sure equipment is safe to use and mandatory posters and signs are present.
The EHO will also inspect for things like gaps and cracks where pests can get in and broken ceiling tiles which could cause debris to fall into food.
The EHO will take samples of food and take photographs of any concerns they have as evidence.
<u>After the inspection</u>
The EHO will get any samples taken tested for harmful food-borne bacteria and report any results.
The EHO will give the establishment its new Food Hygiene Rating.
The EHO will advise the establishment on how to improve their hygiene (if needed), e.g. do more staff training.
The EHO might impose fines / take legal action / close the establishment if there's a high risk to public health.
The EHO might need to give evidence in court in cases where the risk to public health is high.
[Banded mark question — 8 marks available. See page 67 for advice on how to mark your answer.]

(e) You may have included some of these points in your answer:
A Food Hygiene Rating of 2 might give the care home a poor reputation and mean the care home may struggle to attract residents, especially if the low Food Hygiene Rating is reported in the local news or on social media.
The rating may mean the care home struggles to attract staff and damage staff morale, which may reduce staff performance.
Existing residents and/or their relatives may worry about the establishment's food hygiene and safety, which may cause some residents to leave.
This would also impact the business negatively as a smaller number of residents may cause the care home to struggle to make enough money and it may have to close.
[Banded mark question — 4 marks available. See page 67 for advice on how to mark your answer.]

Pages 47-50: The Ramsden Hotel

2 (a) (i) Any four from: e.g. Swimming lessons or children's swim times could be offered in the pool. / The hotel could host parent and baby/toddler groups in the conference rooms. / The café or restaurants could offer a children's menu. / The golf course could offer family golf sessions/lessons. / Conference and banqueting rooms could be made available to hire for parties.
[4 marks available — 1 mark for each suggestion]

(ii) Any four from: e.g. Discounted rates for playing golf/ golf club membership. / Discounted spa/pool use during weekdays. / Fitness classes during weekdays. / Pensioner portions available in café and restaurant/discounted meals/ specials. / Adequate accessible parking in car park near entrance. / Adequate accessibility to all areas, e.g. ramps, lifts. / Banqueting suite available for party hire (e.g. retirement, special birthdays).
[4 marks available — 1 mark for each suggestion]

(iii) Any four from: e.g. Corporate packages and discounts on hotel rooms, dining and conference rooms. / Access to high speed internet with good Wi-Fi coverage. / Desks with convenient plug sockets in hotel rooms. / Access to projectors and sufficient plug sockets for chargers in conference rooms. / Access to an iron/laundry service for work clothing. / 24-hour room service/vending machines to cater for people arriving/leaving outside of restaurant opening hours.
[4 marks available — 1 mark for each suggestion]

For part (a) there are lots of more general answers that you could give (e.g. good parking, range of meal options for different diets, express check-in/out) but these are only likely to get a mark once across all three question parts. To get a mark you need to make sure each way you suggest meets the needs of the specific customer too.

(b) E.g.
Find out as much information about the client's requirements as she can so she can deliver an event that they are happy with.
Keep costs as low as possible so she can charge a competitive price which the client feels is good value for money.
Get an accurate number of guests and details of any dietary needs from the client well in advance of the event, so there's enough time to buy and prepare enough suitable food.
[6 marks available. For each recommendation — 1 mark for a basic recommendation or 2 marks for a more developed recommendation]
There are lots of other points you could include for this answer. For example, use only trustworthy suppliers who are likely to deliver on time, brief all staff working at the event properly before the event takes place and make sure suitable equipment is available, such as highchairs.

(c) (i) buffet service ***[1 mark]***
If you gave another type of counter service as your answer (e.g. cafeteria service) that's still worth a mark here.

(ii) Your answer for this part should be relevant to the answer you gave for part (c) (i). You may have included some of the following points in your answer:

A buffet can provide a wide selection of both hot and cold foods.
Food can be specially-prepared and set aside for students with dietary requirements, allergies and intolerances.
Information about individual foods can be provided with clear labels showing allergens and whether something is vegan or vegetarian so students can identify what they can safely eat.
A buffet will take up less time than table service as there's no waiting for orders to be taken or for food to be delivered.
The cost of a buffet is likely to be lower than the cost of a table-service meal because fewer serving staff will be needed.
[Banded mark question — 4 marks available. See page 67 for advice on how to mark your answer.]

(d) (i) You may have included some of these points in your answer:
The staff should immediately alert guests and begin evacuation.
Staff should tell guests to leave their belongings as taking them with them would slow down the evacuation.
Staff should remind wheelchair users that they can't use lifts as this would be dangerous. If necessary, they should help them to escape (e.g. using evacuation chairs).
Only trained staff or fire marshals should use equipment such as evacuation chairs.
There could be small children and babies in the restaurant, so staff should be prepared to offer parents assistance with evacuating children from the building, especially if they need to be carried.
Staff may need to assist elderly guests to use the stairs.
Staff should check areas such as the toilets and staff-only areas to make sure everyone is evacuated.
Once out of the building, the staff should take guests to the fire assembly point and stay outside.
Staff should identify any missing staff/guests and give this to the fire service along with any other information about the site when they arrive.
Staff should not let anyone re-enter the building until the fire service say it is safe to do so.
[Banded mark question — 8 marks available. See page 67 for advice on how to mark your answer.]

(ii) E.g. The fire should be reported under RIDDOR to the Health and Safety Executive (HSE) because it is classed as a dangerous event that could've caused serious injury or death. ***[2 marks for a well developed outline like this, 1 mark if your answer is more basic]***

Pages 51-53: The Forge

3 (a) You may have included some of these points in your answer:
A vegetable chef is a mid-level chef in the kitchen brigade. / They will take orders from the sous-chef and head chef and work alongside the other chefs de partie. / They are mainly responsible for preparing vegetables for the main dishes and cooking vegetable dishes, as well as soups, stocks and eggs. / If they are experienced, they might have to train up less experienced chefs such as the commis chefs. / The vegetable chef will also have to monitor stock levels of ingredients for their dishes so the restaurant does not run out. / Generally, the vegetable chef must also make sure they follow the Health and Safety at Work Act (HASAWA) to keep themselves safe at work, such as using knives properly. / They also need to follow food safety guidelines and maintain excellent food hygiene levels to prevent cross-contamination.
[Banded mark question — 4 marks available. See page 67 for advice on how to mark your answer.]

(b) You may have included some of these points in your answer:
When the kitchen brigade work together and help each other out on busy stations, this can get food ready to serve more quickly. For example, if the meat chef has lots of orders and the vegetable chef is free, they could help out on the meat station to get through the orders faster.
Effective communication between different members of the kitchen brigade should help make sure the correct food is made and customers receive the correct orders.
If the brigade don't work as a team, mistakes are more likely to be made with orders which could lead to customer complaints and poor reviews.
Working as a team will make sure standards remain high, customers get the correct food on time and leave good reviews. This could help the restaurant to continue to attract customers and contribute to a sense of pride among the staff, which helps motivate them.
Staff that feel well-supported by other members of the kitchen brigade are likely to be more motivated, which might make them more productive.
Supportive coworkers will be beneficial for the mental health of staff.
[Banded mark question — 6 marks available. See page 67 for advice on how to mark your answer.]

(c) (i) You may have included some of these points in your answer:
With a permanent full-time contract, the vegetable chef can expect a steady income each month. This allows the chef to plan their finances more easily than if they were on a part-time, seasonal or zero hours contract.
Having a consistent income each month might help the chef to be less stressed about their finances, which could be beneficial for their mental health.
With a permanent full-time contract, the vegetable chef can also expect paid holidays. This allows them to take time away from work and have a healthy work-life balance.
With a permanent full-time contract, the vegetable chef will also receive sick pay. This means they don't need to worry about loss of income if they get ill and can still financially support themselves.
With a permanent full-time contract, the vegetable chef can expect their employer to contribute to their pension. This will mean they are better-off financially after retirement.
This type of contract provides greater job security than other employment contracts, as they have rights and cannot be dismissed without fair warning.
With a permanent full-time contract, the vegetable chef will have a fixed number of hours to work each week all-year-round so they can have a better work-life balance.
With a full-time contract, the chef would earn more money than if they were only employed part-time.
Being employed on a permanent full-time contract might mean the chef is given more access to training and career progression opportunities than if they were only part-time or temporary.
[Banded mark question — 6 marks available. See page 67 for advice on how to mark your answer.]

(ii) You may have included some of these points in your answer:
Offering the job as a permanent full-time role might help attract the best people who are looking for job security.
It should help to build a stable team who work well together and deliver excellent food efficiently.
Having permanent staff members should increase the likelihood of training being a longer-term investment.
Having a vegetable chef on a permanent full-time contract ensures consistency and reliability in staffing, as the chef is committed to the restaurant on an ongoing basis.
This reduces the need for frequent hiring and training of new staff, which saves time for the restaurant owner and potentially money too (e.g. spending on advertising jobs).
The permanent contract also means the owner can budget for staff wages, pension contributions and plan for annual holiday requests.

A permanent vegetable chef is likely to be more invested in the success of the restaurant, leading to higher levels of dedication and loyalty. This can result in higher quality service and consistency in food preparation, contributing to overall customer satisfaction.
[Banded mark question — 6 marks available. See page 67 for advice on how to mark your answer.]

(d) You may have included some of these points in your answer:
The AA Rosettes will show potential customers that the food and service at The Forge is excellent. This is likely to increase demand from customers as they want to try the excellent food. A boost in customers can increase the revenue/profit that the restaurant makes.
The increased income may allow the The Forge to invest money back into the business to increase standards and make the restaurant even more desirable for customers to visit.
The Forge may also be able to increase their prices and customers will be happy to pay more as they know it will be a high-quality experience, which will increase revenue further.
Gaining AA Rosettes might allow the restaurant to attract top talent as chefs will be drawn to work in a kitchen that's achieved this award. Attracting top talent is likely to help The Forge raise standards even more and work towards achieving another AA Rosette, which could help the business to be even more successful.
Achieving AA Rosettes recognises the hard work of the staff, so it could help boost morale and keep them happy and working hard to maintain high standards.
[Banded mark question — 6 marks available. See page 67 for advice on how to mark your answer.]

(e) E.g. An establishment can achieve a Michelin star. Restaurants can be awarded between one and three Michelin stars depending on the excellence of their food.
An establishment can receive an award from the Good Food Guide. The Good Food Guide gives out awards such as 'Best Local Restaurant'.
[4 marks available. For each award — 2 marks for a well developed outline like one of these, 1 mark if your answer is more basic]
The Food Standards Agency also give all food establishments a rating for their food hygiene. This isn't really an 'award' though so that's why it's not given in the example answer above.

Pages 54-55: Running Rhino Bakery

4 (a) (i) You may have included some of these points in your answer:
Deliveries enter the kitchen next to the storage areas, so high risk food spends less time in danger zone.
Deliveries enter the kitchen next to the storage areas, which avoids bringing dirt from outside into the kitchen.
The serving area is the opposite side of the cooking island from the preparation area. This means that cooked food doesn't go near the raw preparation area again.
The waste area is outside, which reduces the risk of it attracting pests into the kitchen which could lead to physical contamination.
The staff toilets are next to the kitchen meaning staff members are more likely to have just washed their hands when they come back into the kitchen, which should keep the chance of cross-contamination low.
The storage areas are next to the food preparation and cooking areas so ingredients can be picked up and put back quickly. This helps to maintain safe food storage as refrigerated/frozen ingredients are in the danger zone for as little time as possible.
[Banded mark question — 4 marks available. See page 67 for advice on how to mark your answer.]

(ii) You may have included some of these points in your answer:
The staff room is a separate space so staff can take proper breaks. This means they can get away from their work space and rest properly to maintain their mental health.
The staff room is close to the kitchen, so staff are more likely to take their breaks in the staff area. It's important that staff members rest to maintain their mental health.
There's an in/out door system to the dining area which ensures staff don't bump into each other and avoids risk of scalding when staff are carrying hot food/drinks.
The storage areas are next to the food preparation and cooking areas so staff don't have to move too far to gather ingredients, which reduces chances of them tripping or bumping into someone carry something hot.
There is more than one exit from the kitchen which is important if staff need to evacuate in an emergency such as a fire.
The washing and cleaning station is located away from main food preparation and cooking area, which minimises the risk of wet floors that can lead to staff slipping and falling.
[Banded mark question — 4 marks available. See page 67 for advice on how to mark your answer.]

(b) E.g.
Piece of equipment: industrial standing mixer
Justification: E.g. A large standing mixer can help chefs make large batches of cake batter, bread dough, etc. in less time than making by hand or with small standing mixers.
Piece of equipment: large industrial oven
Justification: E.g. An industrial oven can fit more inside it than a smaller domestic oven, which reduces the amount of time it takes to cook a large amount of food.
[6 marks available — 1 mark for each piece of equipment, 1 mark for a basic justification, 2 marks for a more developed justification]
Examples of other pieces of equipment you might've suggested include: a bain-marie, a blast chiller or a proofing cabinet.

(c) Any one from: e.g. By allowing more food to be cooked/prepared in a day, this means the bakery could have more food to sell and therefore make more money. / Each member of staff may be able to prepare/cook more food in a given time period, which might mean the bakery can reduce the number of hours some staff members work/reduce number of staff employed which would reduce wage costs.
[2 marks for a well developed outline like one of these, 1 mark if your answer is more basic]

Pages 56-57: Dunes Caravan Park

5 (a) You may have included some of these points in your answer:
I think that both Steven and the member of staff that asked him to use the meat slicer are at fault.
Steven shouldn't have been asked to use the machine, but also Steven should have refused.
Dunes Caravan Park are also at fault because they should give all staff training in all equipment that they are going to be using.
Steven's accident happened because he was asked to use a dangerous machine he wasn't trained to use.
[Banded mark question — 4 marks available. See page 67 for advice on how to mark your answer.]

(b) Any four from: e.g. Dunes could make sure that all staff are trained on equipment that they might need to use even if it's not something they'd be likely to use regularly. / Dunes could make sure that the risk assessments for all equipment state that staff should only use equipment they've been trained to use. / Dunes could make sure that mandatory health and safety signs and posters are displayed near the meat slicer. / Dunes could update the health and safety training for new staff so that all staff are made aware of the dangers of equipment like the meat slicer. / Dunes could make sure they have staff with the correct training working to carry out all of the tasks required on that shift. / Dunes could hire more staff or give more staff members training to ensure staff with the correct mix of training are on shift when required. / The head chef could take items off the menu that require the use of the meat slicer if there is no appropriately-trained staff member available to use it.
[4 marks available — 1 mark for each recommendation]

(c) Any four from: e.g. All new staff must be trained in meat slicer operation. / Recently trained staff must operate equipment under supervision of head/sous/senior chef. / Refresher training for staff members as and when required. / Check safety guards are in good repair daily. / Maintenance must be carried out annually and recorded. / Kill switch/emergency stop switch must be installed. / Provide PPE (cut resistant gloves) for machine operator. / Keep work area free of clutter. / Lock machine blade when not in use.
[4 marks available — 1 mark for each sensible control measure]

(d) E.g. They should run manual handling training and make sure all staff members involved in moving the meat slicer have attended.
They should also provide staff with carrying equipment, such as a trolley, and/or PPE (e.g. steel toe-capped shoes) if necessary.
[2 marks for a well developed outline like one of these, 1 mark if your answer is more basic]

Pages 58-59: Cactus Summer Camp

6 (a) You may have included some of these points in your answer:
The majority of children have no dietary needs, so meals should follow the latest government guidelines for a healthy, balanced diet (e.g. the Eatwell Guide).
The canteen staff should order a smaller amount of specific ingredients to substitute in meals for those with dietary needs, so they get the right balance of nutrients.
Meals should be based on starchy carbohydrates (like pasta and potato) and contain lots of fruit and vegetables.
Meals should contain some protein, such as meat, fish, eggs, pulses or dairy.
The canteen should avoid offering too many foods that are high in fat or sugar, to promote healthy eating habits.
There should be a variety of options, so all children can choose something to eat, including hot food (e.g. roast dinners) and cold food (e.g. sandwiches).
There are 8 vegetarian children, but vegetarian options should be offered anyway. The canteen can use plant-based sources of protein or use meat substitutes for dishes such as stir fry and lasagne.
There are 6 vegan children, who can't eat meat or animal products. Many vegetarian options would be suitable, such as vegetable-based pasta dishes with tomato sauce.
There are 10 lactose intolerant children who will need dairy substitutes in meals. The canteen staff could use dairy-free butter and cheese in all meals, or use substitutes such as coconut milk or soya milk in specific dishes.
There are 4 gluten intolerant children. The canteen could use cornflour to thicken sauces instead of wheat flour, and offer gluten-free breads and biscuits.
There are 4 children with a nut allergy, which can be fatal. Therefore the canteen could introduce a nut-free policy, so there is zero risk of contamination in dishes.
Meals should be affordable to keep costs down for parents, particularly those on low incomes.
The canteen staff should clearly labels meals with allergens, e.g. with colour-coding, so children can be confident choosing something that isn't harmful to them.
[Banded mark question — 8 marks available. See page 67 for advice on how to mark your answer.]

(b) Any four from: e.g. swelling of throat or tongue / breathing difficulties / tightness in throat / wheezing or coughing / weakness / feeling faint / itchy rash / bloating / vomiting / diarrhoea / anaphylactic shock
[4 marks available — 1 mark for each symptom]

(c) You may have included some of these points in your answer:
Have separate preparation and serving areas for children with allergies.
Use coloured utensils and chopping boards for different allergens.
Make children with allergies collect meals earlier than the other children.
Make sure staff have up-to-date training on food safety.
Store allergenic ingredients in sealed and labelled containers, separate to other ingredients.
Make sure utensils are washed between use and work surfaces sanitised regularly.
Train staff in regular and thorough hand washing between preparing dishes.
Introduce a nut-free policy, to prevent the risk of nuts contaminating other dishes.
Remove ingredients entirely where possible that are known to cause anaphylaxis in surveyed children or staff.
[Banded mark question — 6 marks available. See page 67 for advice on how to mark your answer.]

Pages 60-61: Westoe

7 (a) E.g.
Retired people: bed and breakfast (B&B)
B&Bs are often in quieter locations than hotels, so may be more suitable for retired people.
Families with young children: self-catering lodge
Lodges have lots of facilities, such as a kitchen, which could be used to prepare and store milk for babies.
Young adults: Airbnb
Young adults are likely to have less disposable income, so an Airbnb may be a more affordable option.
There are lots of possible answers here — you may have mentioned cost, equipment, facilities, accessibility, etc.
[6 marks available — 1 mark for each type of accommodation, 1 mark for each justification]

(b) Any two from: e.g. employees will have no income after the season ends unless they find another job / employees may receive few benefits (such as sick pay) / employees have no guarantee of a job the following season / employees have little career progression
[2 marks available — 1 mark for each disadvantage]

(c) You may have included some of these points in your answer:
Restaurants and bistros would have a variety of dishes to cater for the family's tastes, and they should have a children's menu. They offer table service, which is ideal for the parents, because they can supervise their children without having to go up to the counter.
Food stalls/food trucks at the beach would be convenient, as the family would not have to pack up and leave the beach to get food.
Cafés have a relaxed atmosphere and offer lighter meals suitable for children. Many cafés have highchairs or changing facilities that may be needed for the one year old.
Fast food restaurants are quick and would be low cost, which may be important for the family who may have to buy five meals.
Play centres with a café/restaurant would allow the parents to sit and have a meal whilst their children play.
Accessibility and parking is also a consideration — the family are likely to have a pram, so nearby parking and ramp access to an establishment might be important.
[Banded mark question — 6 marks available. See page 67 for advice on how to mark your answer.]

Pages 62-63: Hoad House

8 (a) Any four from: e.g. Upgrade all the rooms to en-suite / include baths in the majority of en-suite rooms. / Invest in high-quality room furnishings and decor, such as bed linen. / Provide more in-room amenities, such as high-speed internet and smart TVs. / Offer enhanced services, such as porters to deliver luggage to rooms. / Offer a wider restaurant menu, with more gourmet options and dishes to cater for dietary needs. / Create a seasonal menu, using high-quality ingredients from local suppliers. / Have a guest feedback system to gather opinions and continuously improve the experience. / Arrange regular training to make sure staff are knowledgeable and can provide a high-quality service. / Ensure staff are well-presented.
[4 marks available — 1 mark for each suggestion]

(b) You may have included some of these points in your answer:
The guest house will receive more publicity and have a higher profile, so more people will be aware of them.
They will be able to charge more for bookings, which could increase revenue and potentially profits too.
There will be a greater demand for bookings and the guest house will likely be fully booked most of the time. This could also mean the guest house makes increased revenue/profit.
They will attract top talent, such as chefs or front of house staff, who will bring experience and new ideas to generate more revenue for the guest house.
They may receive awards and be entered into competitions that could further increase their reputation.
There may be upselling opportunities, such as menu tasting experiences, which could generate more revenue for the guest house.
The staff are likely to feel proud to work for the guest house, who will want to continue to maintain high standards.
[Banded mark question — 6 marks available. See page 67 for advice on how to mark your answer.]

(c) (i) Any three from: e.g. use locally-sourced toiletries / replace single-use toiletries with refillable dispensers or eco-friendly, biodegradable options / offer guests the option to reuse towels and linens to reduce laundry loads / fully load washing machines to reduce water consumption / switch off lights when leaving a room / recycle waste items left in rooms
[3 marks available — 1 mark for each suggestion]

(ii) Any three from: e.g. provide guests with reusable water bottles and encourage them to refill bottles at designated water stations / encourage guests to use eco-friendly ways of travelling in the local area, such as bike rentals or public transport / encourage guests to check-in online to reduce paper usage / encourage recycling among staff and guests by providing clearly labelled bins
[3 marks available — 1 mark for each suggestion]

(iii) Any three from: e.g. use locally-sourced foods / compost food scraps where possible to fertilise home grown crops to use in dishes / offer vegetarian and vegan options alongside meat dishes to cater to environmentally-conscious guests / fully load dishwashers to reduce water consumption / rotate stock (FIFO) to reduce food waste / donate any unused food / reuse containers for storage, e.g. plastic tubs and glass bottles / make soups and stocks from unused vegetables / put lids on pans to reduce energy consumption
[3 marks available — 1 mark for each suggestion]

Pages 64-65: Biddick Hotel and Spa

9 (a) E.g. Printed media / broadcast media
[2 marks available — 1 mark for each form]

(b) You may have included some of these points in your answer:
<u>Advantages</u>
Social media can reach a wide audience quickly and attract new customers to the hotel.
Social media can be used to target specific groups of people who may be interested in visiting the hotel.
Social media is often free, so using it wouldn't add much to marketing costs (there will be labour costs for creating and updating social media posts).
Social media offers, competitions and discounts can generate excitement and boost bookings.
Positive reviews and positive comments made in response to posts can attract new customers.
<u>Disadvantages</u>
Keeping social media up-to-date can be time-consuming and therefore costly.
Keeping social media up-to-date also requires staff with the appropriate skills/training.
Social media is less suitable for reaching some groups, e.g. elderly people.
Social media offers, competitions and discounts could mean the hotel makes less profit.
Negative comments on social media posts or poor online reviews can be seen by a lot of people, harming the reputation of the business and putting people off visiting.
<u>Conclusion</u>
E.g. Biddick Hotel and Spa should use social media. The likely positive impact of social media increasing awareness of the hotel outweighs the risks associated with negative reviews. Not using social media risks them losing bookings to other hotels that do use it.
[Banded mark question — 8 marks available. See page 67 for advice on how to mark your answer.]
This is an evaluate question so forming a conclusion is REALLY important. You might have concluded that they shouldn't touch social media with a bargepole — that's fine, as long as you back it up with reasons.

(c) Any two from: e.g. good communicator / approachable / hardworking / organised / attention to detail / leadership qualities ***[2 marks available — 1 mark for each quality]***

(d) (i) E.g. The number of new customers will decrease because the reputation of the hotel will be damaged.
[2 marks available — 1 mark for an impact, 1 mark for a linked explanation]

(ii) You may have included some of these points in your answer:
Offer some ground floor rooms that can only be reserved by people with disabilities.
Adapt more rooms with accessibility features such as handles, emergency cords and lowered beds.
Install ramps or lifts to allow wheelchair access.
Install a pool lift/hoist for disabled access to the pool.
Make parking spaces near the entrance wider, which can be reserved by people with disabilities.
Provide Braille signs for blind people and audio induction loops for hearing-impaired people.
[Banded mark question — 6 marks available. See page 67 for advice on how to mark your answer.]

Page 66: Rose and Crown Inn

10 (a) Any two from: e.g. An online booking system through a website or an app would allow guests to book rooms at a time convenient to them. / A self-service touch screen at reception would allow guests to check in by themselves even when staff are busy serving other customers. / An automatic text to a guest's phone when booking would mean they have correct details and confirmation to hand when they check in.
[4 marks available — 1 mark for each way, 1 mark for each linked explanation]

(b) You may have included some of these points in your answer:
An EPOS system could reduce mistakes because waiting staff wouldn't need to write orders neatly for David to read.
An EPOS system would mean that orders couldn't be lost by waiting staff.
An EPOS system would allow waiting staff to send orders straight to David, which would mean a more efficient service.
An EPOS system could be used to flag when dishes are no longer available and shouldn't be ordered, so waiting staff can inform their guests.
[Banded mark question — 4 marks available. See page 67 for advice on how to mark your answer.]

HKWQ41